Pint Size Traditions

by Lynette Jensen

Pint Size Traditions *is a collection of favorite* **Thimbleberries** *designs downsized to create charming small quilts. They are delightful gifts and heirlooms, and always fit in any decor.* **Pint Size** *quilts add unique handcrafted charm, color, and texture to small spaces for seasonal touches and special holidays.*

SUN PORCH BASKET
3

ALPINE STAR WALL QUILT
8

ALPINE STAR PINT SIZE
14

BROWN BASKET
18

CLIMBING VINES
22

CORNER FLOWER
28

FLOWERS IN BLOOM
34

GLORY BE
40

HARVEST TIME
44

LOG CABIN PINES
52

BEAR PAW
58

PANSY SQUARE
64

REINDEER TRAIL
70

SNOW TREATS
80

SUNFLOWER GLORY
86

TABLE TOPPER SQUARE
92

WINTER WINDS
96

TEA TIME
101

PINE BERRIES
106

GENERAL INSTRUCTIONS
114

Sun Porch Basket

Sun Porch & Basket

27-inches square

FABRICS AND SUPPLIES

1/3 yard BEIGE PRINT for foundation applique squares and borders

1/8 yard DARK GREEN for basket appliques

6-inch square DARK PURPLE for flower appliques

6-inch square LIGHT PURPLE for flower appliques

6-inch square GOLD PRINT for flower appliques

6-inch square LIGHT GREEN PRINT for leaf appliques

3/4 yard FLORAL for alternate blocks, side and
corner triangles, and borders

1/3 yard GREEN PRINT for binding

7/8 yard backing fabric

quilt batting, at least 31-inches square

paper-backed fusible web

tear away fabric stabilizer for applique (optional)

pearl cotton or machine- embroidery thread
in matching or accent colors for decorative stitches

Basket Blocks

Make 4 blocks

Cutting

From **BEIGE PRINT**:
- Cut 1, 6 x 42-inch strip.
  From the strip cut:
  4, 6-inch applique foundation squares

Applique - Fusible Web Method

Step 1 Position the fusible web, paper side up, over the applique shape. With a pencil, trace the shape onto fusible web the number of times indicated on the pattern pieces, leaving a small margin between each shape. Cut the shapes apart.

Step 2 Following the manufacturer's instructions, fuse the shapes to the wrong side of the fabric chosen for the appliques. Let the fabric cool and cut along the traced line. Peel away the paper backing from the fusible web.

Step 3 Referring to the quilt diagram, position the shapes on the 6-inch **BEIGE** squares; fuse in place.

Note: We suggest pinning a rectangle of tear-away stabilizer to the backside of the block to be appliqued so that it will lay flat when the applique is complete. We use the extra-light-weight Easy Tear™ sheets as a stabilizer. When the applique is complete, tear away the stabilizer.

Step 4 We machine buttonhole-stitched around the shapes using black Mettler® embroidery thread for the top thread and regular sewing thread in the bobbin. If you like, you could hand buttonhole-stitch around the shapes with pearl cotton.

Hand-Buttonhole Stitch Tip

To prevent the buttonhole-stitches from "rolling off" the edges of the appliques, take an extra back-stitch in the same place as you made the buttonhole-stitch, going around outer curves, corners, and points. For straight edges, taking a back-stitch every inch is enough.

Buttonhole Stitch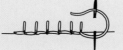

Quilt Center

Note: The side and corner triangles are larger than necessary and will be trimmed before the borders are added.

Cutting
*Note: Refer to **Cutting Side and Corner Triangles** on page 116.*

From **FLORAL**:
- Cut 1, 10-1/2 x 42-inch strip.
  From the strip cut:
  1, 10-1/2-inch square. Cut the square diagonally into quarters for a total of 4 side triangles.
  2, 6-inch squares. Cut the squares in half diagonally for a total of 4 corner triangles.
  1, 6-inch alternate block square

Quilt Center Assembly

Step 1 Referring to the quilt diagram for block placement, sew the appliqued basket blocks, alternating block, and side triangles together in diagonal rows. Press the seam allowances toward the **FLORAL** fabric so the seams will fit snugly together with less bulk.

Step 2 Pin the rows at the block intersections, and sew the rows together. Press the seam allowances in one direction.

Step 3 Sew the corner triangles to the quilt center; press.

Step 4 Trim away the excess fabric from the side and corner triangles, taking care to allow a 1/4-inch seam allowance beyond the corners of each block. Refer to **Trimming Side and Corner Triangles** on page 6 for complete instructions.

Flower
Trace 12
onto
fusible web

Leaf
Trace 8
onto
fusible web

Trimming Side and Corner Triangles

Begin at a corner by lining up your ruler 1/4-inch beyond the points of the corners of the blocks as shown. Cut along the edge of the ruler. Repeat this procedure on all four sides of the quilt top.

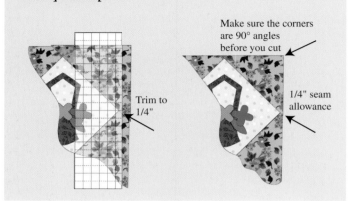

Make sure the corners are 90° angles before you cut

Trim to 1/4"

1/4" seam allowance

Putting It All Together

Trim the backing and batting so they are 4-inches larger than the quilt top. Refer to **Finishing the Quilt** on page 118 for complete instructions.

Binding

Cutting

From **GREEN PRINT**:
- Cut 3, 2-3/4 x 42-inch strips

Sew the binding to the quilt using a 3/8-inch seam allowance. This measurement will produce a 1/2-inch wide finished double binding. Refer to **Binding** and **Diagonal Piecing** on page 119 for complete instructions.

Borders

Note: *The yardage given allows for the border strips to be cut on the crosswise grain. Read through* **Border** *instructions on page 118 for general instructions on adding borders.*

Cutting

From **BEIGE PRINT**:
- Cut 2, 1-1/2 x 42-inch inner border strips
- Cut 2, 1 x 42-inch middle border strips

From **FLORAL**:
- Cut 2, 1 x 42-inch middle border strips
- Cut 3, 3-1/2 x 42-inch outer border strips

Attaching the Borders

Step 1 Attach the 1-1/2-inch wide **BEIGE** inner border strips.

Step 2 Attach the 1-inch wide **FLORAL** middle border strips.

Step 3 Attach the 1-inch wide **BEIGE** middle border strips.

Step 4 Attach the 3-1/2-inch wide **FLORAL** outer border strips.

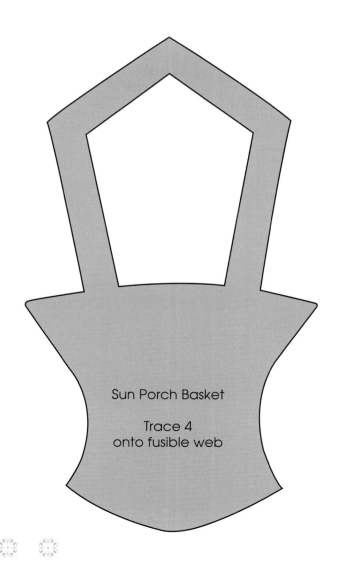

Sun Porch Basket

Trace 4
onto fusible web

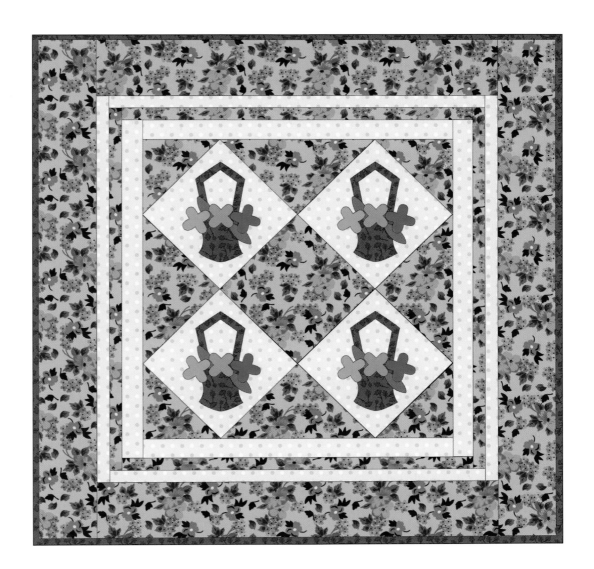

Sun Porch Basket
27-inches square

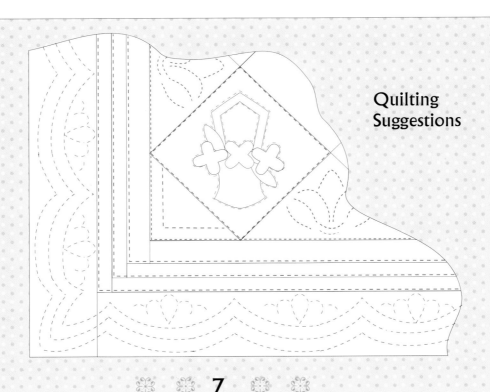

Quilting
Suggestions

Alpine Star Wall Quilt

Alpine & Star

Wall Quilt

35 x 43-inches

FABRICS AND SUPPLIES

1/4 yard each of 3 GREEN PRINTS for trees

7/8 yard BEIGE PRINT for background

1/2 yard GOLD PRINT for star

1/8 yard BROWN PRINT for tree trunks

3/4 yard CHESTNUT FLORAL for border

1/4 yard RED PRINT for corner squares

1/2 yard GREEN PLAID for binding (cut on the bias)

1-1/3 yards backing fabric

quilt batting, at least 39 x 47-inches

Tree Blocks

Make 3 blocks

Cutting

From **each GREEN PRINT**:
- Cut 1, 4-1/2 x 8-1/2-inch rectangle
- Cut 6, 2-1/2 x 8-1/2-inch rectangles

From **BEIGE PRINT**:
- Cut 4, 4-1/2 squares
- Cut 3, 2-1/2 x 42-inch strips.
  From the strips cut: 36, 2-1/2-inch squares
- Cut 2, 3-1/2 x 16-inch strips

From **GOLD PRINT**:
- Cut 2, 4-1/2-inch squares

From **BROWN PRINT**:
- Cut 1, 2-1/2 x 16-inch strip

Piecing

Step 1 With right sides together, position a 4-1/2-inch **BEIGE** square on the corner of a 4-1/2 x 8-1/2-inch **GREEN** rectangle. Draw a diagonal line on the square and stitch on the line. Trim seam allowance to 1/4-inch; press. Repeat this process at the opposite corner of the rectangle.

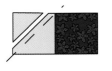

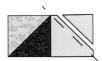

Make 1 unit from 2 of the **GREEN PRINT** fabrics

Step 2 With right sides together, position a 4-1/2-inch **GOLD** square on the corner of a 4-1/2 x 8-1/2-inch **GREEN** rectangle. Draw a diagonal line on the square. Stitch, trim, and press. Repeat this process at the opposite corner of the rectangle.

Make 1

Step 3 With right sides together, position a 2-1/2-inch **BEIGE** square on both corners of a 2-1/2 x 8-1/2-inch **GREEN** rectangle. Draw a diagonal line on the squares, stitch, trim, and press.

Make 6 units from each of the 3 **GREEN PRINT** fabrics

Step 4 Sew the corresponding tree units together as shown in Step 6. Press the seam allowances in opposite directions for ease in joining the trees together. Make 3 trees.

Step 5 Sew the 3-1/2 x 16-inch **BEIGE** strips to both side edges of the 2-1/2 x 16-inch **BROWN** strip; press. Cut the strip set into segments.

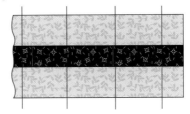

Cut 3, 4-1/2-inch wide segments

Step 6 Add a trunk unit to the bottom of each tree; press. <u>At this point each tree should measure 8-1/2 x 20-1/2-inches.</u> Referring to the quilt diagram, sew the 3 trees together, positioning the tree with the **GOLD** triangles in the center; press.

Make 1 tree block from 2 of the **GREEN PRINT** fabrics

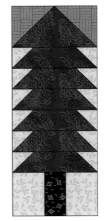

Make 1 tree block from 1 of the **GREEN PRINT** fabrics

Star Block

Cutting

From **GOLD PRINT**:
- Cut 1, 8-1/2-inch square
- Cut 6, 4-1/2-inch squares

From **BEIGE PRINT**:
- Cut 2, 4-1/2 x 42-inch strips.
  - From the strips cut:
    - 3, 4-1/2 x 8-1/2-inch rectangles
    - 2, 4-1/2-inch squares
    - 2, 4-1/2 x 12-1/2-inch rectangles

Piecing

Step 1 With right sides together, position a 4-1/2-inch **GOLD** square on the corner of a 4-1/2 x 8-1/2 **BEIGE** rectangle. Draw a diagonal line on the square, stitch, trim, and press. Repeat this process at the opposite corner of the rectangle.

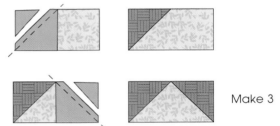

Make 3

Step 2 Sew a Step 1 unit to both side edges of the 8-1/2-inch **GOLD** square; press. Sew 4-1/2-inch **BEIGE** squares to both side edges of the remaining Step 1 unit; press. Sew the units together; press. Sew the 4-1/2 x 12-1/2-inch **BEIGE** rectangles to both edges of the star block; press.

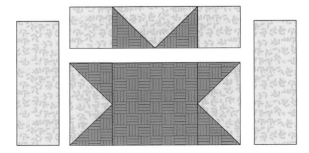

Step 3 Referring to the quilt diagram, sew the star unit to the top edge of the tree unit; press.

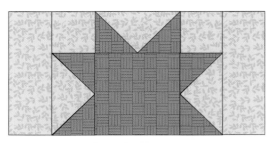

Border

Note: *The yardage given allows for the border strips to be cut on the crosswise grain. Read through **Border** instructions on page 118 for general instructions on adding borders.*

Cutting

From **CHESTNUT FLORAL**:
- Cut 4, 5-1/2 x 42-inch border strips

From **RED PRINT**:
- Cut 4, 5-1/2-inch corner squares

Attaching the Border

Step 1 Attach the 5-1/2-inch wide **CHESTNUT FLORAL** top and bottom border strips.

Step 2 For the side borders, measure the quilt from top to bottom through the middle, including the seam allowances but not the top/bottom borders. Cut 2, 5-1/2-inch wide **CHESTNUT FLORAL** border strips to this length. Sew a 5-1/2-inch **RED** corner square to both ends of the border strips; press. Sew the borders to the quilt center; press.

Putting It All Together

Trim the backing fabric and batting so they are 4-inches larger than the quilt top. Refer to **Finishing the Quilt** on page 118 for complete instructions.

Binding

Cutting

From **GREEN PLAID**:
- Cut enough 2-3/4-inch wide **bias** strips to make a 170-inch long strip.

Sew the binding to the quilt using a 3/8-inch seam allowance. This measurement will produce a 1/2-inch wide finished double binding. Refer to **Binding** and **Diagonal Piecing** on page 119 for complete instructions.

Alpine Star Wall Quilt
35 x 43-inches

Picture This
Suggestions for Creative Pint Size Quilt Displays

Frame with traditional frames and mat board

• To keep quilts perfectly square and in place, stitch the quilt to mat using a large darning needle and quilting thread. Hide the stitches in the ditch between the quilt and the binding. Just a few stitches at each corner and then every two inches or so will hold quilt firmly in place. Use a carpenter's square to help align the quilt. It is not necessary to knot and tie off between stitched areas. The long stretches of thread are hidden nicely on the back of the mat.

• Choose a frame that allows for the thickness of your quilt. Any quality good framing shop can guide you in your choice. A framed quilt with glass turns a little quilt into a work of art.

Use unusual, unexpected items to mount a small quilt for a visual treat

Consider these suggestions . . .
- A vintage window screen
- A section of weathered fencing
- A vintgage garden gate
- An interesting cupboard door
- A framed panel of old ceiling tin

Alpine Star

Pint Size

18 x 22-inches

FABRICS AND SUPPLIES

1/8 yard each of 3 GREEN PRINTS for trees

1/3 yard BEIGE PRINT for background

1/4 yard GOLD PRINT for star

2 x 10-inch piece BROWN PRINT for tree trunks

1/4 yard RED FLORAL for border

1/8 yard BLACK PRINT for corner squares

3/8 yard GREEN PLAID for binding (cut on the bias)

5/8 yard backing fabric

quilt batting, at least 22 x 26-inches

Tree Blocks

Make 3 blocks

Cutting

From **each GREEN PRINT**:
- Cut 1, 2-1/2 x 4-1/2-inch rectangle
- Cut 6, 1-1/2 x 4-1/2-inch rectangles

From **BEIGE PRINT**:
- Cut 1, 2-1/2 x 42-inch strip.
  From the strip cut:
  4, 2-1/2-inch squares
  2, 2 x 9-inch strips
- Cut 2, 1-1/2 x 42-inch strips.
  From the strips cut:
  36, 1-1/2-inch squares

From **GOLD PRINT**:
- Cut 2, 2-1/2-inch squares

From **BROWN PRINT**:
- Cut 1, 1-1/2 x 9-inch strip

Piecing

Step 1 With right sides together, position a 2-1/2-inch **BEIGE** square on the corner of a 2-1/2 x 4-1/2-inch **GREEN** rectangle. Draw a diagonal line on the square and stitch on the line. Trim seam allowance to 1/4-inch; press. Repeat this process at the opposite corner of the rectangle.

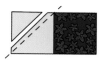 

Make 1 unit from 2 of the **GREEN PRINT** fabrics

Step 2 With right sides together, position a 2-1/2-inch **GOLD** square on the corner of a 2-1/2 x 4-1/2-inch **GREEN** rectangle. Draw a diagonal line on the square. Stitch, trim, and press. Repeat this process at the opposite corner of the rectangle.

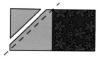 

Make 1

Step 3 With right sides together, position a 1-1/2-inch **BEIGE** square on both corners of a 1-1/2 x 4-1/2-inch **GREEN** rectangle. Draw a diagonal line on the squares, stitch, trim, and press.

Make 6 units from each of the 3 **GREEN PRINT** fabrics

Step 4 Sew the corresponding tree units together as shown in Step 6. Press the seam allowances in opposite directions for ease in joining the trees together. Make 3 trees.

Step 5 Sew the 2 x 9-inch **BEIGE** strips to both side edges of the 1-1/2 x 9-inch **BROWN** strip; press. Cut the strip set into segments.

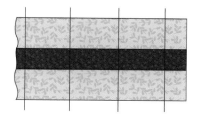

Cut 3, 4-1/2-inch wide segments

Step 6 Add a trunk unit to the bottom of each tree; press. At this point each tree should measure 4-1/2 x 10-1/2-inches. Referring to the quilt diagram, sew the 3 trees together, positioning the tree with the **GOLD** triangles in the center; press.

Make 1 tree block from 2 of the **GREEN PRINT** fabrics

Make 1 tree block from 1 of the **GREEN PRINT** fabrics

Star Block

Cutting

From **GOLD PRINT**:
- Cut 1, 4-1/2-inch square
- Cut 6, 2-1/2-inch squares

From **BEIGE PRINT**:
- Cut 1, 2-1/2 x 42-inch strip.
    From the strip cut:
    2, 2-1/2 x 6-1/2-inch rectangles
    3, 2-1/2 x 4-1/2-inch rectangles
    2, 2-1/2-inch squares

Piecing

Step 1 With right sides together, position a 2-1/2-inch **GOLD** square on the corner of a 2-1/2 x 4-1/2-inch **BEIGE** rectangle. Draw a diagonal line on the square, stitch, trim, and press. Repeat this process at the opposite corner of the rectangle.

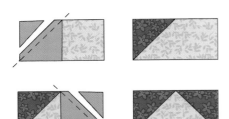

Make 3

Step 2 Sew a Step 1 unit to both side edges of the 4-1/2-inch **GOLD** square; press. Add 2-1/2-inch **BEIGE** squares to both side edges of the remaining Step 1 unit; press. Sew the units together; press. Sew the 2-1/2 x 6-1/2-inch **BEIGE** rectangles to both edges of the star block; press.

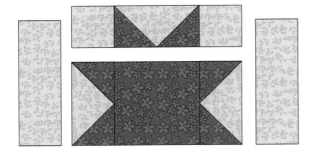

Step 3 Referring to the quilt diagram, sew the star unit to the top edge of the tree unit; press.

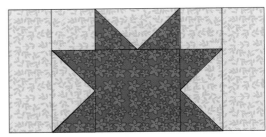

Border

Note: The yardage given allows for the border strips to be cut on the crosswise grain. Read through **Border** instructions on page 118 for general instructions on adding borders.

Cutting

From **RED FLORAL**:
- Cut 2, 3-1/2 x 42-inch strips

From **BLACK PRINT**:
- Cut 4, 3-1/2-inch corner squares

Attaching the Border

Step 1 Attach the 3-1/2-inch wide **RED FLORAL** top and bottom border strips.

Step 2 For the side borders, measure the quilt from top to bottom through the middle, including the seam allowances but not the top/bottom borders. Cut 2, 3-1/2-inch wide **RED FLORAL** border strips to this length. Sew a 3-1/2-inch **BLACK** corner square to both ends of the border strips; press. Sew the borders to the quilt center; press.

Putting It All Together

Trim the backing fabric and batting so they are 4-inches larger than the quilt top. Refer to **Finishing the Quilt** on page 118 for complete instructions.

Binding

Cutting

From **GREEN PLAID**:
• Cut enough 2-3/4-inch wide **bias** strips to make a 90-inch long strip.

Sew the binding to the quilt using a 3/8-inch seam allowance. This measurement will produce a 1/2-inch wide finished double binding. Refer to **Binding** and **Diagonal Piecing** on page 119 for complete instructions.

Alpine Star
18 x 22-inches

Brown Basket

Brown & Basket

20-1/2-inches square

FABRICS AND SUPPLIES

1/4 yard RED PRINT for basket block and middle border

1/4 yard BROWN PRINT for basket block and corner squares

1/4 yard BEIGE PRINT for basket block

1/4 yard BEIGE FLORAL for center square, and side and corner triangles

1/4 yard DARK BROWN PRINT for inner border and corner squares

1/4 yard GREEN FLORAL for outer border and corner squares

1/4 yard DARK BROWN PRINT for binding

3/4 yard fabric for quilt backing

quilt batting, at least 25-inches square

Basket Blocks

Make 4 blocks

Cutting

From **RED PRINT**:
- Cut 1, 1-7/8 x 22-inch strip

From **BROWN PRINT**:
- Cut 1, 2-7/8 x 10-inch strip.
  From the strip cut 2, 2-7/8-inch squares.
  Cut the squares in half diagonally to make
  4 triangles.
- Cut 1, 1-7/8 x 15-inch strip
- Cut 4, 7/8 x 4-1/2-inch **bias** strips

From **BEIGE PRINT**:
- Cut 1, 2-7/8 x 10-inch strip. From the strip cut:
  2, 2-7/8-inch squares. Cut the squares in half
  diagonally to make 4 triangles.
- Cut 1, 2-1/2 x 15-inch strip. From the strip cut:
  8, 1-1/2 x 2-1/2-inch rectangles
- Cut 1, 1-7/8 x 42-inch strip. From the strip cut:
  1, 1-7/8 x 22-inch strip
  1, 1-7/8 x 15-inch strip

Step 1 With right sides together, layer the 1-7/8 x
22-inch **BEIGE** and **RED** strips. Press together, but
do not sew. Cut the layered strip into squares.
Cut the layered squares in half diagonally to
make 20 sets of triangles. Stitch 1/4-inch from
the diagonal edge of each pair of triangles;
press. At this point each triangle-pieced square
should measure 1-1/2-inches square.

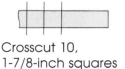

Crosscut 10,
1-7/8-inch squares

Make 20, 1-1/2-inch
triangle-pieced squares

Step 2 In the same manner, layer together the
BROWN and **BEIGE** 1-7/8 x 15-inch strips. Cut the
layered strip into 6, 1-7/8-inch squares. Cut the
squares in half diagonally and stitch to make 12,
1-1/2-inch triangle-pieced squares.

Make 12, 1-1/2-inch
triangle-pieced squares

Step 3 To make the basket handles, fold
each **BROWN** 7/8-inch wide strip in half
lengthwise with wrong sides together; press.
To keep the raw edges aligned, stitch a scant
1/4-inch away from the edges. Fold the strip
in half again so the raw edges are hidden by
the first folded edge; press. Hand-baste if
needed.

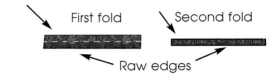

First fold   Second fold

Raw edges

Step 4 Position the handles on the **BEIGE**
triangles. The folded edge of the handle
should be 1/2-inch from the raw edge of the
triangle. Pin handle in place and miter corner. Hand applique 4 handle triangles with
matching thread.

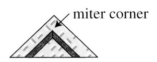

miter corner

Step 5 Referring to the block diagram for
color placement, assemble the triangle-
pieced squares, 1-1/2 x 2-1/2-inch **BEIGE**
rectangles, **BROWN** triangles, and handle
triangles.

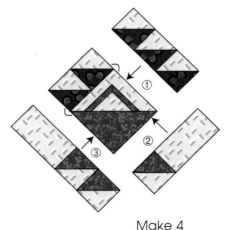

Make 4

Sew the pieces
together in
sections as
shown. Sew
the sections
together to
form a block.
At this point
each block
should measure
4-1/2-inches
square.

Quilt Center

Note: The side and corner triangles are larger than necessary and will be trimmed before the border is attached.

Cutting

From **BEIGE FLORAL**:
- Cut 1, 7-1/2 x 42-inch strip. From the strip cut:
  1, 7-1/2-inch square. Cut the square into quarters diagonally to make 4 side triangles.
  2, 5-1/2-inch squares. Cut the squares in half diagonally to make 4 corner triangles.
  1, 4-1/2-inch square for center block

Quilt Center Assembly

Step 1 Sew the blocks and side triangles together in diagonal rows; press. The corner triangles are added last.

Step 2 Trim away the excess fabric from the side and corner triangles, leaving a 1/4-inch seam allowance beyond the block corners. Refer to **Trimming Side and Corner Triangles** on page 6 for complete instructions.

Borders and Corner Squares

*Note: The yardage given allows for the border strips to be cut on the crosswise grain. Read through **Border** instructions on page 118 for general instructions on adding borders.*

Cutting

From **DARK BROWN PRINT**:
- Cut 2, 1-1/2 x 42-inch inner border strips
- Cut 4, 2-inch corner squares

From **RED PRINT**:
- Cut 2, 2 x 42-inch middle border strips

From **GREEN FLORAL**:
- Cut 2, 2-1/2 x 42-inch outer border strips
- Cut 4, 1-1/2 corner squares

From **BROWN PRINT**:
- Cut 4, 2-1/2-inch corner squares

Attaching the Borders

Step 1 Attach the 1-1/2-inch wide **DARK BROWN** top and bottom inner border strips.

Step 2 For the side inner borders, measure the quilt from top to bottom through the middle, including the seam allowances but not the top/bottom borders. Cut 2, 1-1/2-inch wide **DARK BROWN** border strips to this length. Sew a 1-1/2-inch **GREEN FLORAL** corner square to both ends of the border strips; press. Sew the borders to the quilt center; press.

Step 3 Attach the 2-inch wide **RED** top and bottom middle border strips.

Step 4 For the side middle borders, refer to Step 2 to attach the 2-inch wide **RED** border strips with 2-inch **DARK BROWN** corner squares.

Step 5 Attach the 2-1/2-inch wide **GREEN FLORAL** top and bottom outer border strips.

Step 6 For the side outer borders, refer to Step 2 to attach the 2-1/2-inch wide **GREEN FLORAL** border strips with 2-1/2-inch **BROWN** corner squares.

Putting It All Together

Trim the backing fabric and batting so they are 4-inches larger than the quilt top. Refer to **Finishing the Quilt** on page 118 for complete instructions.

Binding

Cutting

From **DARK BROWN PRINT**:
- Cut 3, 2-3/4 x 42-inch strips

Sew the binding to the quilt using a 3/8-inch seam allowance.

This measurement will produce a 1/2-inch wide finished double binding. Refer to **Binding** and **Diagonal Piecing** on page 119 for complete instructions.

Climbing Vines

Climbing & Vines

40-inches square

FABRICS AND SUPPLIES

1-1/8 yards GREEN FLORAL for pieced blocks and outer border

5/8 yard BEIGE PRINT #1 for pieced blocks

1/4 yard DARK RED PRINT for inner border and flower appliques

1/4 yard BEIGE PRINT #2 for middle border

1/8 yard MEDIUM RED PRINT for flower center appliques

1/8 yard GREEN PRINT #1 for leaf appliques

1/3 yard GREEN PRINT #2 for vine appliques

1/2 yard DARK RED PRINT for binding

1-1/4 yards backing fabric

quilt batting, at least 44-inches square

freezer paper for appliques

Pieced Blocks

Make 16 blocks

Cutting

From **GREEN FLORAL**:
- Cut 1, 3-7/8 x 42-inch strip.
    From the strip cut:
    8, 3-7/8-inch squares. Cut the squares
    in half diagonally to make
    16 large triangles.
- Cut 1, 2-3/8 x 42-inch strip.
    From the strip cut:
    16, 2-3/8-inch squares. Cut the squares
    in half diagonally to make
    32 small triangles.
- Cut 2 more 2-3/8 x 42-inch strips

From **BEIGE PRINT #1**:
- Cut 2, 6-7/8 x 42-inch strips.
    From the strips cut:
    8, 6-7/8-inch squares. Cut the squares
    in half diagonally to make 16 triangles.
- Cut 2, 2-3/8 x 42-inch strips
- Cut 1, 2 x 42-inch strip. From the strip cut:
    16, 2-inch squares

Piecing

Step 1 With right sides together, layer the
2-3/8 x 42-inch **GREEN FLORAL** and **BEIGE #1**
strips together in pairs. Press together, but do
not sew. Cut the layered strips into squares.
Cut the layered squares in half diagonally to
make 64 sets of triangles. Stitch 1/4-inch from
the diagonal edge of each pair of triangles;
press. At this point each triangle-pieced
square should measure 2-inches square.

Crosscut 32, 2-3/8-inch squares

Make 64, 2-inch
triangle-pieced squares

Step 2 Sew the triangle-pieced squares
together in pairs; press.

Unit A   Unit B
Make 16   Make 16

Step 3 Sew the A units to the top edge of the
GREEN FLORAL large triangles; press.

Unit A

Make 16

Step 4 Sew the 2-inch **BEIGE #1** squares to the
edge of the B units; press. Sew these units to
the left edge of the Step 3 units; press. Add
GREEN FLORAL small triangles to both ends of
the units; press.

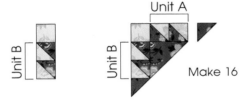

Unit A

Unit B   Unit B

Make 16

Step 5 Sew the large **BEIGE #1** triangles to the
Step 4 units; press. At this point each pieced
block should measure 6-1/2-inches square.

Make 16

Step 6 Sew 4 of the pieced blocks together to
form the quilt center; press. Using a removable
fabric marker or a quilter's silver pencil, draw a
5-1/2-inch circle very lightly over the center of
these blocks to be used as a placement guide
for the center vine.

Quilt Center

Cutting

From **GREEN PRINT #2**:
• Cut enough 1-1/2-inch wide **bias** strips to make a 20-inch long strip for the center vine

Appliqueing the Center Vine

Step 1 Diagonally piece the **GREEN #2 bias** strips together, referring to **Diagonal Piecing** on page 118 for complete instructions.

Step 2 To make the vine, fold the **GREEN #2** strip in half lengthwise with wrong sides together; press. To keep the raw edges aligned, stitch a scant 1/4-inch away from the edges. Fold the strip in half again so the raw edges are hidden by the first folded edge; press. Hand-baste if needed.

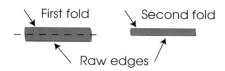

First fold   Second fold
Raw edges

Step 3 Position the prepared vine on the drawn circle in the middle of the quilt center and hand-baste or pin in place. Machine- or hand-applique the vine in place.

Center Leaf Applique - Freezer Paper Method

Step 1 Make a template using the leaf shape on page 27. Use a pencil to trace the shape 12 times on the paper side of the freezer paper and cut out the shapes on the traced lines.

Step 2 With a hot, dry iron, press the coated side of the freezer paper shapes onto the wrong side of the fabric chosen for the applique. Allow at least 1/2-inch between each shape for seam allowances.

Step 3 Cut out the shapes a scant 1/4-inch beyond the edge of the freezer paper pattern.

Step 4 Position and pin the leaves along the center vine. With your needle, turn the seam allowances over the edge of the freezer paper and hand-applique in place. When there is about 3/4-inch left to applique, slide your needle into this opening, loosen the freezer paper from the fabric, and gently pull the freezer paper out. Finish stitching the applique in place.

Quilt Center Assembly

Step 1 Sew 8 of the pieced blocks together in pairs; press.

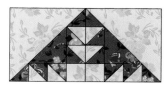

Make 4 pairs

Step 2 Referring to the quilt assembly diagram, sew a pair of pieced blocks to the top/bottom edges of the appliqued quilt center; press. Sew the remaining pieced blocks to both ends of the 2 remaining pairs of pieced blocks; press. Sew these units to both side edges of the quilt center; press. At this point the quilt center should measure 24-1/2-inches square.

Borders

*Note: The yardage given allows for the border strips to be cut on the crosswise grain. Diagonally piece the strips as needed, referring to **Diagonal Piecing** instructions on page 118. Read through **Border** instructions on page 118 for general instructions on adding borders.*

Cutting

From **DARK RED PRINT**:
- Cut 3, 1 x 42-inch inner border strips

From **BEIGE PRINT #2**:
- Cut 3, 2 x 42-inch middle border strips

From **GREEN FLORAL**:
- Cut 4, 6-1/2 x 42-inch outer border strips

Attaching the Borders

Step 1 Attach the 1-inch wide **DARK RED** inner border strips.

Step 2 Attach the 2-inch wide **BEIGE #2** middle border strips.

Step 3 The additional applique shapes can be added at this time (see **Applique the Quilt Top** below).

Step 4 Attach the 6-1/2-inch wide **GREEN FLORAL** outer border strips.

Applique the Quilt Top

Cutting

From **GREEN PRINT**:
- Cut enough 1-1/2-inch wide **bias** strips to make 4, 24-inch long strips for the corner vines

Applique the Vines, Flowers, and Leaves

Step 1 Prepare the vines in the same manner as the quilt center vine.

Step 2 Referring to the quilt diagram for placement, position the 4 corner vines on the **BEIGE #1** corner units making sure the center circles are 3-inches in diameter so the flowers will fit inside them. Pin and hand-baste the corner vines in place. Hand-applique the vines to the quilt top. The short ends of the vines will be covered by the leaves, so there is no need to turn them under.

Step 3 Using the freezer applique method, prepare the flower and leaf appliques for the corner units and outer border in the same manner as the quilt center leaf appliques on page 27. Trace the leaf shapes 32 times and the A flower and B flower center shapes 4 times.

Step 4 Position and pin the flowers, flower centers, and leaves on the quilt top. Hand-applique the shapes in place in the same manner as the quilt center leaf appliques, layering as needed.

Putting It All Together

Trim the backing and batting so they are 4-inches larger than the quilt top. Refer to **Finishing the Quilt** on page 118 for complete instructions.

Binding

Cutting

From **DARK RED PRINT**:
- Cut 5, 2-3/4 x 42-inch strips

Sew the binding to the quilt using a 3/8-inch seam allowance. This measurement will produce a 1/2-inch wide finished double binding. Refer to **Binding** and **Diagonal Piecing** on page 119 for complete instructions.

Climbing Vines
40-inches square

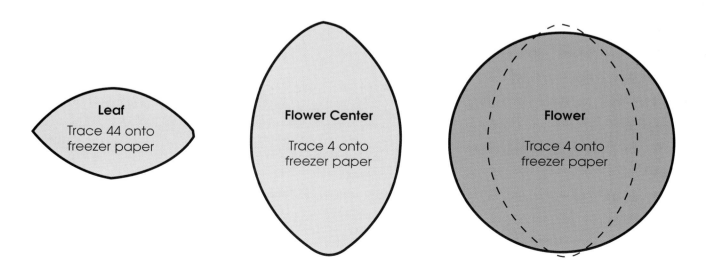

Leaf

Trace 44 onto
freezer paper

Flower Center

Trace 4 onto
freezer paper

Flower

Trace 4 onto
freezer paper

Corner Flower

Corner Flower & Wall Quilt

35 x 43-inches

FABRICS AND SUPPLIES

1/3 yard RED PRINT for flowers and first middle border

3/4 yard BEIGE PRINT for background, side and corner triangles

1/4 yard GOLD PRINT for flowers and second middle border

1/3 yard GREEN PRINT for leaves and inner border

7/8 yard RED FLORAL for outer border

3/8 yard GOLD PRINT for binding

1-1/3 yards backing fabric

quilt batting, at least 39 x 48-inches

Corner Flower Blocks

Make 6 blocks

Cutting

From RED PRINT:
- Cut 5, 1 x 42-inch strips.
    From the strips cut:
    48, 1 x 1-1/2-inch rectangles
    96, 1-inch squares

From BEIGE PRINT:
- Cut 3, 1-1/2 x 42-inch strips.
    From the strips cut:
    24, 1-1/2 x 3-inch rectangles
    24, 1-1/2-inch squares
- Cut 4, 1 x 42-inch strips.
    From the strips cut:
    96, 1 x 1-1/2-inch rectangles

From GOLD PRINT:
- Cut 1, 1-1/2 x 42-inch strip.
    From the strip cut:
    24, 1-1/2-inch squares

From GREEN PRINT:
- Cut 3, 1 x 42-inch strips.
    From the strips cut:
    24, 1 x 2-inch rectangles
    24, 1 x 2-1/2-inch rectangles
- Cut 6, 1-1/2-inch squares

Piecing

Step 1 Position a 1-inch **RED** square on the corner of a 1 x 1-1/2-inch **BEIGE** rectangle. Draw a diagonal line on the **RED** square, and stitch on the line. Trim the seam allowance to 1/4-inch; press. Repeat this process at the opposite corner of the rectangle. Sew a 1 x 1-1/2-inch **RED** rectangle to the bottom of the unit; press. At this point each unit should measure 1-1/2-inches square.

Make 48   Make 48

Step 2 Sew together a 1-1/2-inch **BEIGE** square, a 1-1/2-inch **GOLD** square, and 2 of the Step 1 units; press. At this point each unit should measure 2-1/2-inches square.

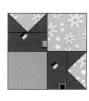

Make 24

Step 3 Position a 1 x 1-1/2-inch **BEIGE** rectangle on the corner of a 1 x 2-inch **GREEN** rectangle. Draw a diagonal line on the **BEIGE** rectangle, stitch, trim; and press. Sew the leaf unit to the left edge of the Step 2 unit; press.

  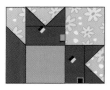

Make 24

Make 24

Step 4 In the same manner, position a 1 x 1-1/2-inch **BEIGE** rectangle on the corner of a 1 x 2-1/2-inch **GREEN** rectangle. Draw a diagonal line, stitch, trim; press. Sew the leaf unit to the bottom edge of the Step 3 unit; press. At this point each flower unit should measure 3-inches square.

  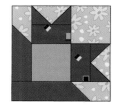

Make 24

Make 24

Step 5 Referring to the block diagram, sew flower units to both side edges of a 1-1/2 x 3-inch **BEIGE** rectangle; press. Make 12 units.

Step 6 Referring to the block diagram, sew a 1-1/2 x 3-inch **BEIGE** rectangle to both sides of a 1-1/2-inch **GREEN** square; press. Make 6 units.

Step 7 Sew the Step 5 units to the top and bottom edges of the Step 6 units; press. At this point each block should measure 6-1/2-inches square.

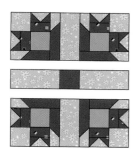 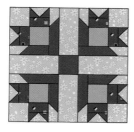

Make 6

Quilt Center

Note: *The side and corner triangles are larger than necessary and will be trimmed before the borders are added.*

Cutting

Note: *Refer to* **Cutting Side and Corner Triangles** *on page 116.*

From **BEIGE PRINT**:
- Cut 1, 10-1/2 x 42-inch strip.
   From the strip cut:
   2, 10-1/2-inch squares. Cut the squares diagonally into quarters for a total of 8 triangles. You will be using only 6 for side triangles.
- Cut 1, 6-1/2 x 42-inch strip.
   From the strip cut:
   2, 6-1/2-inch alternate blocks
   2, 6-inch squares. Cut the squares in half diagonally for a total of 4 corner triangles.

Quilt Center Assembly

Step 1 Referring to the quilt diagram for placement, sew together the Corner Flower blocks, 6-1/2-inch **BEIGE** alternate blocks, and **BEIGE** side triangles in 4 diagonal rows. Press the seam allowances toward the **BEIGE** alternate blocks and side triangles.

Step 2 Sew the diagonal rows together; press. Add the corner triangles to the quilt center; press.

Step 3 Trim away the excess fabric from the side and corner triangles, taking care to allow a 1/4-inch seam allowance beyond the corners of each block. Refer to **Trimming Side and Corner Triangles** on page 6.

Borders

Note: *The yardage given allows for the border strips to be cut on the crosswise grain. Read through* **Border** *instructions on page 118 for general instructions on adding borders.*

Cutting

From **GREEN PRINT**:
- Cut 3, 1-1/2 x 42-inch inner border strips

From **RED PRINT**:
- Cut 3, 1-1/2 x 42-inch first middle border strips

From **GOLD PRINT**:
- Cut 4, 1-1/2 x 42-inch second middle border strips

From **RED FLORAL**:
- Cut 4, 6-1/2 x 42-inch outer border strips

Attaching the Borders

Step 1 Attach the 1-1/2-inch wide **GREEN** inner border strips.

Step 2 Attach the 1-1/2-inch wide **RED PRINT** first middle border strips.

Step 3 Attach the 1-1/2-inch wide **GOLD** second middle border strips.

Step 4 Attach the 6-1/2-inch wide **RED FLORAL** outer border strips.

Putting It All Together

Trim the backing and batting so they are about 4-inches larger than the quilt top. Refer to **Finishing the Quilt** on page 118 for complete instructions.

Binding

Cutting

From **GOLD PRINT**:
- Cut 4, 2-3/4 x 42-inch strips

Sew the binding to the quilt using a 3/8-inch seam allowance. This measurement will produce a 1/2-inch wide finished double binding. Refer to **Binding** and **Diagonal Piecing** on page 119 for complete instructions.

Corner Flower Wall Quilt
35 x 43-inches

Quilting Suggestion

Trace this quilt template to use on the
Alternate Blocks of Corner Flower

Actual Size

Flowers In Bloom

27-inches square

FABRICS AND SUPPLIES

1/4 yard WINE PRINT for flower blocks

4 x 14-inch rectangle GOLD PRINT for flower centers

1/8 yard RUST PRINT for flower blocks

5/8 yard TAN/WINE FLORAL for flower blocks, pieced border,
and outer border

3/8 yard GREEN PRINT for flower blocks, middle border,
and pieced border

3/8 yard BEIGE PRINT for background, lattice, and inner border

1/3 yard GREEN PRINT for binding

7/8 yard backing fabric

quilt batting, at least 31-inches square

Flower Blocks

Make 4 blocks

Cutting

From **WINE PRINT**:
- Cut 2, 1-1/2 x 42-inch strips.
  From the strips cut:
  8, 1-1/2 x 4-1/2-inch rectangles
  8, 1-1/2 x 2-1/2-inch rectangles
- Cut 1, 1 x 42-inch strip. From the strip cut:
  16, 1-inch squares

From **GOLD PRINT**:
- Cut 4, 2-1/2-inch squares

From **RUST PRINT**:
- Cut 1, 1-1/2 x 42-inch strip.
  From the strip cut:
  16, 1-1/2-inch squares

From **TAN/WINE FLORAL**:
- Cut 3, 1-1/2 x 42-inch strips.
  From the strips cut:
  1, 1-1/2 x 16-inch strip
  24, 1-1/2 x 2-1/2-inch rectangles
  8, 1-1/2-inch squares

From **GREEN PRINT**:
- Cut 3, 1-1/2 x 42-inch strips.
  From the strips cut:
  32, 1-1/2 x 2-1/2-inch rectangles
  16, 1-1/2-inch squares

From **BEIGE PRINT**:
- Cut 5, 1-1/2 x 42-inch strips.
  From the strips cut:
  1, 1-1/2 x 16-inch strip
  8, 1-1/2 x 3-1/2-inch rectangles
  24, 1-1/2 x 2-1/2-inch rectangles
  48, 1-1/2-inch squares

Piecing

Step 1 Position 1-inch **WINE** squares on the corners of a 2-1/2-inch **GOLD** square. Draw a diagonal line on each square and stitch on the lines. Trim the seam allowances to 1/4-inch; press.

Make 4

Step 2 Sew 1-1/2 x 2-1/2-inch **WINE** rectangles to the top/bottom of each unit; press.

Step 3 Position 1-1/2-inch **GREEN** squares on both corners of a 1-1/2 x 4-1/2-inch **WINE** rectangle. Draw a diagonal line on each square, stitch, trim, and press. Make 8 units. Sew the units to the side edges of the Step 2 units; press. <u>At this point each flower center should measure 4-1/2-inches square</u>.

Make 4 flower centers

Make 8

Step 4 Aligning long edges, sew the 1-1/2 x 16-inch **BEIGE** and **TAN/WINE FLORAL** strips together; press. Cut the strip set into segments.

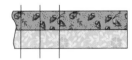

Crosscut 8, 1-1/2-inch wide segments

Step 5 Position a 1-1/2-inch **BEIGE** square on the left corner of a 1-1/2 x 2-1/2-inch **GREEN** rectangle. Draw a diagonal line on the square, stitch, trim, and press.

Make 32

Step 6 Position a 1-1/2-inch **BEIGE** square on the left corner of a 1-1/2 x 2-1/2-inch **TAN/WINE FLORAL** rectangle. Draw a diagonal line on the square, stitch, trim, and press. Repeat this process at the right corner of the rectangle, using a 1-1/2-inch **RUST** square.

Make 16

Step 7 Position a 1-1/2-inch **TAN/WINE FLORAL** square on the left corner of a 1-1/2 x 2-1/2-inch **BEIGE** rectangle. Draw a diagonal line on the square, stitch, trim, and press. Sew a 1-1/2 x 2-1/2-inch **BEIGE** rectangle to the top edge of the unit; press.

Make 8   Make 8

Step 8 Position a 1-1/2 x 2-1/2-inch **TAN/WINE FLORAL** rectangle on the left corner of a 1-1/2 x 2-1/2-inch **BEIGE** rectangle. Draw a diagonal line on the **TAN/WINE FLORAL** rectangle, stitch, trim, and press. Sew a 1-1/2 x 3-1/2-inch **BEIGE** rectangle to the top edge of the unit; press.

Make 8   Make 8

Step 9 Sew together 2 of the Step 5 units, a Step 6 unit, and a Step 4 segment; press. Make 8 sections. Sew the sections to the top/bottom edges of the Step 3 flower center section; press.

Make 8

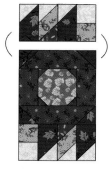

Make 4

Step 10 Sew together a Step 7 unit, 2 of the Step 5 units, a Step 6 unit, and a Step 8 unit; press. Make 8 sections. Sew the sections to the side edges of the Step 9 section; press. <u>At this point each flower block should measure 8-1/2-inches square.</u>

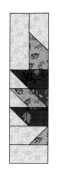  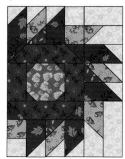

Make 8   Make 4

Quilt Center

Cutting

From **BEIGE PRINT**:
- Cut 3, 1-1/2 x 42-inch strips.
  From the strips cut:
  2, 1-1/2 x 19-1/2-inch side inner border strips
  3, 1-1/2 x 17-1/2-inch lattice/inner border strips
  2, 1-1/2 x 8-1/2-inch lattice strips

Quilt Center Assembly

Step 1 Referring to the quilt diagram, sew the flower blocks to both side edges of the 1-1/2 x 8-1/2-inch **BEIGE** lattice strips; press. Make 2 block rows.

Step 2 Sew together the block rows and the 3, 1-1/2 x 17-1/2-inch **BEIGE** lattice/inner border strips; press. Sew the 1-1/2 x 19-1/2-inch **BEIGE** side inner border strips to the quilt center; press.

Borders

Note: *The yardage given allows for the border strips to be cut on the crosswise grain. Diagonally piece the strips as needed, referring to **Diagonal Piecing** instructions on page 118. Read through **Border** instructions on page 118 for general instructions on adding borders.*

Cutting

From **GREEN PRINT**:
- Cut 3, 1-1/2 x 42-inch strips.
  From the strips cut:
  28, 1-1/2 x 3-1/2-inch rectangles
- Cut 2 more 1-1/2 x 42-inch strips for middle border

From **TAN/WINE FLORAL**:
- Cut 3, 2-1/2 x 42-inch outer border strips
- Cut 3, 1-1/2 x 42-inch strips.
  From the strips cut:
  60, 1-1/2-inch squares

Attaching the Borders

Step 1 Attach the 1-1/2-inch wide **GREEN** middle border strips.

Step 2 Position 1-1/2-inch **TAN/WINE FLORAL** squares on both corners of a 1-1/2 x 3-1/2-inch **GREEN** rectangle. Draw a diagonal line on the squares, stitch, trim, and press.

Make 28

Step 3 For the top/bottom pieced borders, sew together 7 of the Step 2 units; press. Make 2 border strips. Sew the borders to the quilt center; press.

Step 4 For the side pieced bor-

ders, sew together 7 of the Step 2 units; press. Make 2 border strips. Sew 1-1/2-inch **TAN/WINE FLORAL** squares to both ends of the border strips; press. Sew the borders to the quilt center; press.

Step 5 Attach the 2-1/2-inch wide **TAN/WINE FLORAL** outer border strips.

Putting It All Together

Trim the backing and batting so they are 4-inches larger than the quilt top. Refer to **Finishing the Quilt** on page 118 for complete instructions.

Binding

Cutting

From **GREEN PRINT**:
- Cut 3, 2-3/4 x 42-inch strips

Sew the binding to the quilt using a 3/8-inch seam allowance. This measurement will produce a 1/2-inch wide finished double binding. Refer to **Binding** and **Diagonal Piecing** on page 119 for complete instructions.

Flowers In Bloom
27-inches square

Flowers in Bloom Vertical Wall Quilt

18 x 29-inches

Fabrics and Supplies

1/8 yard **WINE PRINT** for flower blocks

4 x 7-inch rectangle **GOLD PRINT** for flower centers

3 x 15-inch rectangle **RUST PRINT** for flower blocks

3/8 yard **TAN/WINE FLORAL** for flower blocks, pieced border, and outer border

5/8 yard **GREEN PRINT** for flower blocks, middle border, pieced border, and binding

1/3 yard **BEIGE PRINT** for background, lattice, and inner border

5/8 yard backing fabric

quilt batting, at least 22 x 33-inches

- Refer to **Flowers in Bloom** to cut and piece 2 flower blocks.

- From **BEIGE PRINT**:
    Cut 2, 1-1/2 x 42-inch lattice/inner border strips. Sew together the flower blocks and lattice strips; press.
    Sew the inner border strips to the quilt center; press. Read through **Border** instructions on page 118 for general instructions on adding borders.

- From **GREEN PRINT**:
    Cut 2, 1-1/2 x 42-inch strips.
    From the strips cut:
    22, 1-1/2 x 3-1/2-inch rectangles
    Cut 2 more 1-1/2 x 42-inch strips for middle border
    Cut 3, 2-3/4 x 42-inch binding strips

- From **TAN/WINE FLORAL**:
    Cut 3, 2-1/2 x 42-inch outer border strips
    Cut 2, 1-1/2 x 42-inch strips.
    From the strips cut:
    48, 1-1/2-inch squares

- Attach the 1-1/2-inch wide **GREEN** middle border strips.

- Refer to **Borders** on pages 37 and 38 to make 22 units to be used for the pieced borders. For the top/bottom pieced borders, sew together 4 of the units; press. Sew the borders to the quilt center; press. For the side pieced borders, sew together 7 of the units; press. Make 2 border strips. Sew 1-1/2-inch **TAN/WINE FLORAL** squares to both ends of the border strips; press. Sew the borders to the quilt center; press.

- Attach the 2-1/2-inch wide **TAN/WINE FLORAL** outer border strips.

- Trim the backing and batting so they are 4-inches larger than the quilt top. Refer to **Finishing the Quilt** on page 118 for complete instructions.

- Sew the **GREEN** binding to the quilt using a 3/8-inch seam allowance. This measurement will produce a 1/2-inch wide finished double binding. Refer to **Binding** and **Diagonal Piecing** on page 119 for complete instructions.

Glory Be

Glory Be

15 x 18-1/2-inches

FABRICS AND SUPPLIES

4 x 4-1/2-inch rectangle BLUE PLAID for flag

1/8 yard RED PRINT for flag

1/4 yard BEIGE PRINT for flag and star background

2 x 7-inch rectangles of 6 ASSORTED PRINTS for stars

1/8 yard BROWN PRINT for inner border

1/4 yard BLUE PRINT for outer border

1/8 yard RED FLORAL for corner squares

1/2 yard BLUE/GOLD PLAID for binding (cut on the bias)

1/2 yard backing fabric

quilt batting, at least 19 x 22-inches

pearl cotton for decorative stitches: gold

Quilt Center

Cutting

From **BLUE PLAID**:
- Cut 1, 4 x 4-1/2-inch rectangle

From **RED PRINT**:
- Cut 2, 1 x 42-inch strips. From the strips cut:
    3, 1 x 9-1/2-inch strips
    4, 1 x 5-1/2-inch strips

From **BEIGE PRINT**:
- Cut 1, 1-7/8 x 42-inch strip. From the strip cut:
    12, 1-7/8-inch squares
- Cut 1, 1-1/2 x 42-inch strip. From the strip cut:
    24, 1-1/2-inch squares
- Cut 2, 1x 42-inch strips. From the strips cut:
    3, 1 x 9-1/2-inch strips
    3, 1 x 5-1/2-inch strips

From **each** of the **6 ASSORTED PRINTS**:
- Cut 2, 1-7/8-inch squares
- Cut 1, 1-1/2-inch square

Piecing

Step 1 Sew the 1 x 5-1/2-inch **RED** strips and the 1 x 5-1/2-inch **BEIGE** strips together; press. Sew this unit to the 4 x 4-1/2-inch **BLUE PLAID** rectangle; press.

Step 2 Sew the 1 x 9-1/2-inch **RED** strips and the 1 x 9-1/2-inch **BEIGE** strips together; press. Sew this unit to the bottom edge of the Step 1 unit; press. At this point the flag section should measure 7 x 9-1/2-inches.

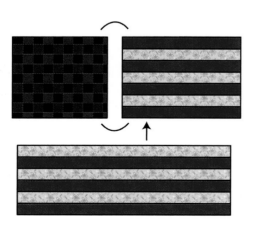

Step 3 Using gold pearl cotton, straight-stitch stars on the **BLUE PLAID** rectangle.

Star Straight Stitch

Step 4 With right sides together, layer a 1-7/8-inch **BEIGE** square and a 1-7/8-inch square from one of the **ASSORTED PRINT** fabrics. Cut the layered square in half diagonally to make the 2 sets of triangles. Stitch a 1/4-inch from the diagonal edge of each pair of triangles; press. Repeat with remaining **ASSORTED PRINT** squares to make 4 triangle-pieced squares using each fabric.

Make 4, 1-1/2-inch triangle-pieced squares from each of the assorted fabrics

Step 5 To make a star block, sew 1-1/2-inch **BEIGE** squares to both side edges of 2 of the triangle-pieced squares; press. Sew triangle-pieced squares to both side edges of a 1-1/2-inch **ASSORTED PRINT** square. Sew the 3 sections together to make a star; press. At this point each star block should measure 3-1/2-inches squares.

Make 2   Make 1

Make 1 star from each of the 6 assorted fabrics

Step 6 Sew the 6 star blocks together; press. Sew the star section to the bottom edge of the flag section; press. At this point the quilt center should measure 9-1/2 x 13-inches.

Borders

Note: The yardage given allows for the border strips to be cut on the crosswise grain. Read through **Border** instructions on page 118 for general instructions on adding borders.

Cutting

From **BROWN PRINT**:
- Cut 2, 1-1/2 x 42-inch inner border strips

From **BLUE PRINT**:
- Cut 2, 2-1/2 x 42-inch outer border strips

From **RED PRINT**:
- Cut 4, 2-1/2-inch corner squares

Attaching the Borders

Step 1 Attach the 1-1/2-inch wide **BROWN** inner border strips.

Step 2 Attach the 2-1/2-inch wide top/bottom outer border **BLUE** strips.

Step 3 For the side outer borders, measure the quilt from top to bottom through the middle, including the seam allowances, but not the top/bottom borders. Cut 2, 2-1/2-inch wide **BLUE** side outer border strips to this length. Sew a 2-1/2-inch **RED FLORAL** corner square to both ends of the border strips; press. Sew the border strips to the quilt center; press.

Putting It All Together

Trim the backing fabric and batting so they are 4-inches larger than the quilt top. Refer to **Finishing the Quilt** on page 118 for complete instructions.

Binding

Cutting

From **BLUE/GOLD PLAID**:
- Cut enough 2-3/4-inch wide **bias** strips to make an 80-inch long strip

Sew the binding to the quilt using a 3/8-inch seam allowance. This measurement will produce a 1/2-inch wide finished double binding. Refer to **Binding** and **Diagonal Piecing** on page 119 for complete instructions.

Glory Be
15 x 18-1/2-inches

Harvest Time

44

Harvest Time

34 x 37-inches

Fabrics and Supplies

1/3 yard DARK ORANGE PRINT for pumpkins

1/4 yard MEDIUM ORANGE PRINT for pumpkins

7/8 yard BEIGE PRINT for background

1/4 yard BLACK PRINT for pumpkin stems and middle border

1/3 yard GREEN PRINT #1 for 8 leaves and sawtooth border

1/4 yard BROWN PRINT for 8 leaves

1/8 yard GREEN PRINT #2 for 2 leaves

1/8 yard GOLD PRINT for 6 leaves

5/8 yard PUMPKIN PRINT for outer border

3/8 yard BLACK PRINT for binding

1-1/8 yards backing fabric

quilt batting, at least 38 x 42-inches

Pumpkin Blocks

Make 5 blocks

Cutting

From **DARK ORANGE PRINT**:
- Cut 1, 2-1/2 x 42-inch strip.
  From the strip cut:
  5, 2-1/2 x 6-1/2-inch rectangles
- Cut 3, 1-1/2 x 42-inch strips.
  From the strips cut:
  10, 1-1/2 x 6-1/2-inch rectangles
  20, 1-1/2-inch squares

From **MEDIUM ORANGE PRINT**:
- Cut 3, 1-1/2 x 42-inch strips.
  From the strips cut:
  10, 1-1/2 x 6-1/2-inch rectangles
  20, 1-1/2-inch squares

From **BEIGE PRINT**:
- Cut 1, 3 x 42-inch strip. From the strip cut:
  5, 3 x 3-1/2-inch rectangles
- Cut 1, 2 x 42-inch strip. From the strip cut:
  10, 2 x 3-inch rectangles
  5, 2-inch squares
- Cut 1, 1-1/2 x 42-inch strip. From the strip cut:
  20, 1-1/2-inch squares

From **BLACK PRINT**:
- Cut 1, 2 x 42-inch strip. From the strip cut:
  5, 2 x 3-inch rectangles
  5, 1-1/2 x 2-inch rectangles

Piecing

Step 1 Position a 1-1/2-inch **MEDIUM ORANGE** square on the corner of a 2-1/2 x 6-1/2-inch **DARK ORANGE** rectangle. Draw a diagonal line on the square, and stitch on the line. Trim the seam allowance to 1/4-inch; press. Repeat this process at the remaining 3 corners of the **DARK ORANGE** rectangle.

Make 5

Step 2 Position 1-1/2-inch **BEIGE** squares on the corners of a 1-1/2 x 6-1/2-inch **DARK ORANGE** rectangle. Draw a diagonal line on the squares, stitch, trim, and press.

Make 10

Step 3 Position 1-1/2-inch **DARK ORANGE** squares on the corners of a 1-1/2 x 6-1/2-inch **MEDIUM ORANGE** rectangle. Draw a diagonal line on the squares, stitch, trim, and press.

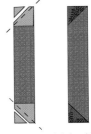

Make 10

Step 4 Referring to the diagram, sew together the Step 1, Step 2, and Step 3 units; press. <u>At this point each pumpkin should measure 6-1/2-inches square.</u>

Make 5

Step 5 Sew the 1-1/2 x 2-inch **BLACK** rectangles and the 2 x 3-inch **BEIGE** rectangles together in pairs; press.

Make 5

Step 6 Position a 2 x 3-inch **BLACK** rectangle on the corner of a 2 x 3-inch **BEIGE** rectangle. Draw a diagonal line on the **BLACK** rectangle, stitch, trim, and press. Position a 2-inch **BEIGE** square on the right corner of the unit. Draw a diagonal line on the **BEIGE** square, stitch, trim, and press.

Make 5

Step 7 Sew a Step 6 unit to the top edge of a Step 5 unit; press. Sew a 3 x 3-1/2-inch **BEIGE** rectangle to the right edge of the unit; press. <u>At this point each pumpkin stem unit should measure 3-1/2 x 6-1/2-inches</u>.

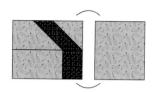

Make 5

If the pumpkin base does not match the stem unit, recheck your measurements and seam allowances. Because so many seams are involved, there is a tendency for the pumpkin base to be a bit smaller than the stem unit. For this reason it is necessary to recheck your seam allowance and make adjustments if needed. <u>Do Not</u> trim down the stem unit.

Step 8 Sew a stem unit to the top edge of a pumpkin unit; press. <u>At this point each pumpkin block should measure 6-1/2 x 9-1/2-inches</u>.

Make 5

Leaf Blocks

Make 8 using **GREEN PRINT #1**
Make 8 using **BROWN PRINT**
Make 6 using **GOLD PRINT**
Make 2 using **GREEN PRINT #2**
(Make a total of 24 leaf blocks)

Cutting

From **GREEN PRINT #1**:
- Cut 2, 2-1/2 x 42-inch strips.
  From the strips cut:
  8, 2-1/2-inch squares
  16, 1-1/2 x 2-1/2-inch rectangles
  8, 3/4 x 2-1/2-inch rectangles for stems

From **BROWN PRINT**:
- Cut 2, 2-1/2 x 42-inch strips.
  From the strips cut:
  8, 2-1/2-inch squares
  16, 1-1/2 x 2-1/2-inch rectangles
  8, 3/4 x 2-1/2-inch rectangles for stems

From **GOLD PRINT**:
- Cut 1, 2-1/2 x 42-inch strip.
  From the strip cut:
  6, 2-1/2-inch squares
  12, 1-1/2 x 2-1/2-inch rectangles
  6, 3/4 x 2-1/2-inch rectangles for stems

From **GREEN PRINT #2**:
- Cut 1, 2-1/2 x 42-inch strip.
  From the strip cut:
  2, 2-1/2-inch squares
  4, 1-1/2 x 2-1/2-inch rectangles
  2, 3/4 x 2-1/2-inch rectangles for stems

From **BEIGE PRINT**:
- Cut 4, 1-1/2 x 42-inch strips.
  From the strips cut:
  96, 1-1/2-inch squares
- Cut 2, 1-3/4 x 42-inch strips.
  From the strips cut:
  24, 1-3/4-inch squares. Cut the squares in half diagonally to make 48 triangles for the stem units.

Piecing

Step 1 To make the **GREEN #1** leaves, position 1-1/2-inch **BEIGE** squares on opposite corners of a 2-1/2-inch **GREEN #1** square. Draw a diagonal line on the **BEIGE** squares, stitch, trim, and press.

Make 8 using
GREEN PRINT #1

Step 2 Position a 1-1/2-inch **BEIGE** square on the right corner of a 1-1/2 x 2-1/2-inch **GREEN #1** rectangle. Draw a diagonal line on the square, stitch, trim, and press.

Make 8 using
GREEN PRINT #1

Step 3 Position a 1-1/2-inch **BEIGE** square on the left corner of a 1-1/2 x 2-1/2-inch **GREEN #1** rectangle. Draw a diagonal line on the square, stitch, trim, and press.

Make 8 using
GREEN PRINT #1

Step 4 For the stem units, center a **BEIGE** triangle on each of the 3/4 x 2-1/2-inch **GREEN #1** rectangles. Stitch a 1/4-inch seam allowance. Center another **BEIGE** triangle on the **GREEN** rectangle, stitch, and press the seam allowances toward the **GREEN** rectangle. The stems will extend beyond the triangles. Trim each stem unit to 1-1/2-inches square.

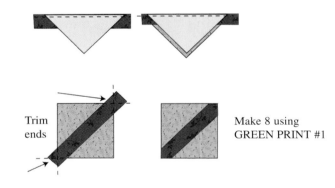

Trim ends

Make 8 using
GREEN PRINT #1

Step 5 Sew the stem units to the left edge of the Step 2 leaf units; press.

Make 8 using
GREEN PRINT #1

Step 6 Sew the Step 3 leaf units to the left edge of the Step 1 leaf units; press.

Make 8 using
GREEN PRINT #1

Step 7 Referring to the block diagram, sew together the Step 5 and Step 6 units; press. At this point each leaf block should measure 3-1/2-inches square.

Make 8 using
GREEN PRINT #1

Step 8 Repeat Steps 1 through 7 to make the remaining leaves.

Make 8 using
BROWN PRINT

Make 6 using
GOLD PRINT

Make 2 using
GREEN PRINT #2

Quilt Center

Assembling the Quilt Center

Referring the the quilt diagram for block placement, sew together 12 leaf blocks and the pumpkin blocks in 3 vertical rows; press. Sew the rows together; press. At this point the quilt center should measure 18-1/2 x 21-1/2-inches.

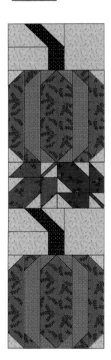 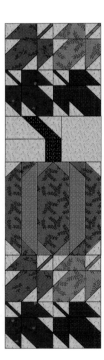 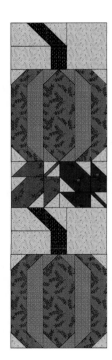

Borders

Note: The yardage given allows for the border strips to be cut on the crosswise grain. Refer to **Finishing the Quilt** on page 118 for complete instructions. Diagonally piece the strips as needed.

Cutting

From GREEN PRINT #1:
- Cut 2, 1-7/8 x 42-inch strips for sawtooth border

From BEIGE PRINT:
- Cut 2, 1-7/8 x 42-inch strips for sawtooth border
- Cut 2, 1-1/2 x 42-inch strips.
  From the strips cut:
    2, 1-1/2 x 15-1/2-inch side inner pieced border strips
    2, 1-1/2 x 12-1/2-inch top/bottom inner pieced border strips
- Cut 3 more 1-1/2 x 42-inch strips for the middle border

From BLACK PRINT:
- Cut 2, 1-1/2 x 42-inch strips.
  From the strips cut:
    2, 1-1/2 x 15-1/2-inch side inner pieced border strips
    2, 1-1/2 x 12-1/2-inch top/bottom inner pieced border strips

From PUMPKIN PRINT:
- Cut 4, 4-1/2 x 42-inch outer border strips

Piecing and Attaching the Borders

Step 1 With right sides together, layer the 1-7/8 x 42-inch **BEIGE** and **GREEN #1** strips, in pairs. Press together, but do not sew. Cut the layered strips into squares. Cut the layered squares in half diagonally to make 54 sets of triangles. Stitch 1/4-inch from the diagonal edge of each pair of triangles; press. <u>At this point each triangle-pieced square should measure 1-1/2-inches square.</u>

Crosscut 27, 1-7/8-inch squares   Make 54, 1-1/2-inch triangle-pieced squares

Step 2 For the top/bottom sawtooth borders, sew together 12 triangle-pieced squares; press. <u>At this point each sawtooth border strip should measure 1-1/2 x 12-1/2-inches.</u> Sew a 1-1/2 x 12-1/2-inch **BEIGE** strip to the top edge and sew a 1-1/2 x 12-1/2-inch **BLACK** strip to the bottom edge of each sawtooth border strip; press.

Step 3 Referring to the diagram for placement, sew a **GOLD** leaf block to the left edge and sew a **BROWN** leaf block to the right edge of the pieced border strips; press. Sew the border strips to the top/bottom edges of the quilt center; press.

Make 2

Step 4 For the side sawtooth borders, sew together 15 triangle-pieced squares; press. <u>At this point each sawtooth border strip should measure 1-1/2 x 15-1/2-inches.</u> Sew a 1-1/2 x 15-1/2-inch **BEIGE** strip to the top edge and sew a 1-1/2 x 15-1/2-inch **BLACK** strip to the bottom edge of each sawtooth border strip; press.

Step 5 Sew a **GOLD** leaf block to the left edge of the pieced border strips; press. Sew a **BROWN** leaf block to the right edge of the pieced border strips; press. Sew **GREEN #1** leaf blocks to both ends of the pieced border strips, referring to the diagram; press. Sew the border strips to the side edges of the quilt center; press.

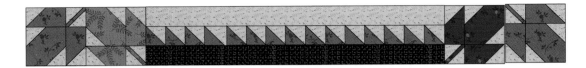

Make 2

Step 6 Attach the 1-1/2-inch wide **BEIGE** inner border strips.

Step 7 Attach the 4-1/2-inch wide **PUMPKIN PRINT** outer border strips.

Putting It All Together

Trim the backing and batting so they are 4-inches larger than the quilt top. Refer to **Finishing the Quilt** on page 118 for complete instructions.

Binding

Cutting

From **BLACK PRINT**:
• Cut 4, 2-3/4 x 42-inch strips

Sew the binding to the quilt using a 3/8-inch seam allowance. This measurement will produce a 1/2-inch wide finished double binding. Refer to **Binding** and **Diagonal Piecing** on page 119 for complete instructions.

Harvest Time
34 x 37-inches

Harvest Time Runner

15 x 36-inches

Fabrics and Supplies

1/3 yard **DARK ORANGE PRINT** for pumpkins
1/4 yard **MEDIUM ORANGE PRINT** for pumpkins
1/4 yard **BEIGE PRINT** for background
1/8 yard **BLACK PRINT** for pumpkin stems
3/8 yard **PUMPKIN PRINT** for border
1/3 yard **BLACK PRINT** for binding
5/8 yard backing fabric
quilt batting, at least 19 x 40-inches

- Refer to **Harvest Time** to cut and piece 5 pumpkin blocks. Sew the pumpkin blocks together; press.

- From **PUMPKIN PRINT**:
  Cut 3, 3-1/2 x 42-inch border strips

- Sew the **PUMPKIN PRINT** border strips to the quilt center; press.

- Trim the backing and batting so they are 4-inches larger than the runner top. Refer to **Finishing the Quilt** on page119 for complete instructions.

- From **BLACK PRINT**:
  Cut 3, 2-3/4 x 42-inch binding strips

- Sew the binding to the quilt using a 3/8-inch seam allowance. This measurement will produce a 1/2-inch wide finished double binding. Refer to **Binding** and **Diagonal Piecing** on page 119 for complete instructions.

Harvest Time Runner
15 x 36-inches

Log Cabin Pines

Log Cabin & Pines

32 x 38-inches

FABRICS AND SUPPLIES

1/4 yard GREEN PRINT #1 for trees

3/4 yard WHEAT PRINT for tree blocks and log cabin blocks

4 x 12-inch rectangle BROWN PRINT for tree trunks

1/8 yard *each* of 3 ASSORTED RED PRINTS for log cabin strips

1/4 yard *each* of 4 ASSORTED GREEN PRINTS for log cabin strips

1/3 yard BLACK PRINT for log cabin center squares and inner border

1-1/8 yards BLACK/TAN PLAID for outer border
(cut on the lengthwise grain)

3/8 yard BLACK/TAN PLAID for binding (cut on the bias)

1-1/8 yards backing fabric

quilt batting, at least 36 x 42-inches

Tree Blocks

Make 6 blocks

Cutting

From **GREEN PRINT #1**:
- Cut 1, 3-1/2 x 42-inch strip.
    From the strip cut:
        6, 3-1/2 x 6-1/2-inch rectangles
- Cut 1, 2-1/2 x 42-inch strip.
    From the strip cut:
        6, 2-1/2 x 6-1/2-inch rectangles

From **WHEAT PRINT**:
- Cut 2, 3-1/2 x 42-inch strips.
    From the strips cut:
        12, 3-1/2-inch squares
        2, 2-1/2 x 11-inch strips
- Cut 1, 2-1/2 x 42-inch strip.
    From the strip cut:
        12, 2-1/2-inch squares

From **BROWN PRINT**:
- Cut 1, 2-1/2 x 11-inch strip

Piecing

Step 1 Position a 3-1/2-inch **WHEAT** square on the corner of a 3-1/2 x 6-1/2-inch **GREEN #1** rectangle. Draw a diagonal line on the **WHEAT** square, and stitch on the line. Trim the seam allowance to 1/4-inch; press. Repeat this process at the opposite corner of the rectangle.

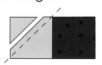
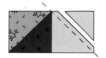

Make 6

Step 2 Position 2-1/2-inch **WHEAT** squares on both corners of a 2-1/2 x 6-1/2-inch **GREEN** rectangle. Draw a diagonal line on the squares, stitch, trim. and press.

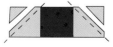

Make 6

Step 3 Aligning long edges, sew the 2-1/2 x 11-inch **WHEAT** strips to both side edges of the 2-1/2 x 11-inch **BROWN** strip; press. Cut the strip set into segments.

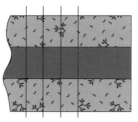

Crosscut 6, 1-1/2-inch wide segments

Step 4 Sew together the Step 1, Step 2, and Step 3 units; press. <u>At this point each tree block should measure 6-1/2-inches square.</u>

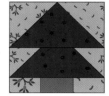

Make 6

Log Cabin Blocks

Make 8 **GREEN** blocks
Make 48 **WHEAT/RED-GREEN** blocks

Cutting

From **BLACK PRINT**:
- Cut 3, 1-1/2 x 42-inch strips.
    From the strips cut:
        56, 1-1/2-inch center squares

From **WHEAT PRINT**:
- Cut 14, 1 x 42-inch strips

From **ASSORTED RED PRINTS**:
- Cut a total of 9, 1 x 42-inch strips

From **ASSORTED GREEN PRINTS**:
- Cut a total of 16, 1 x 42-inch strips

Piecing

Step 1 For the 8 **GREEN** blocks, sew a 1-inch wide **GREEN** strip to a 1-1/2-inch **BLACK** square. Press the seam allowance toward the strip. Trim the strip even with the edge of the center square, creating a two-piece unit.

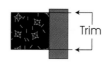

Trim

Make 8

Step 2 Turn the two-piece unit to the right a quarter turn. Stitch a different 1-inch wide **GREEN** strip to the two-piece unit; press and trim.

Step 3 Continue adding 1-inch wide **ASSORTED GREEN** strips to complete the log cabin block. Press and trim each strip before adding the next. <u>Each log cabin block should measure 3-1/2-inches square when completed.</u>

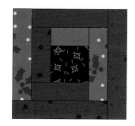

Make 8

Step 4 For the 48 **WHEAT/RED-GREEN** blocks, sew a 1-inch wide **WHEAT** strip to a 1-1/2-inch **BLACK** center square; press and trim.

 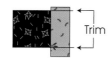

Make 48

Step 5 Turn the two-piece unit to the right a quarter turn. Stitch another 1-inch wide **WHEAT** strip to the two-piece unit; press and trim.

 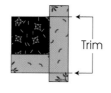

Trim

Step 6 Turn the unit to the right a quarter turn. Stitch a 1-inch wide **RED** or **GREEN** strip to the unit; press and trim. Turn the unit again to the right and add a different 1-inch wide **RED** or **GREEN** strip; press and trim.

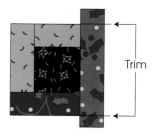

Trim

Step 7
Referring to the block diagram for color placement, continue adding 1-inch wide **WHEAT** strips and **ASSORTED RED** or **GREEN** strips to complete the log cabin block. Press and trim each strip before adding the next. <u>Each log cabin block should measure 3-1/2-inches square when complete.</u>

Make 48

Quilt Center Assembly

Step 1 Refer to the diagrams for color placement and sew the log cabin blocks together in units of 4; press.

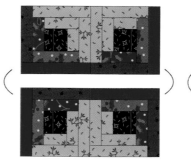 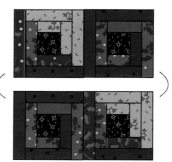

Make 10 log cabin units

Make 4 log cabin corner block units

Step 2 Sew the log cabin units and the tree blocks together in rows. Press the seam allowances in alternating directions by rows so the seams will fit snugly together with less bulk. Pin the blocks at the intersections and sew the rows together; press. At this point the quilt center should measure 24-1/2 x 30-1/2-inches.

Borders

Note: The yardage given allows for the BLACK/TAN PLAID outer border strips to be cut on the lengthwise grain (a couple extra inches are allowed for trimming). Cutting the strips on the lengthwise grain will eliminate the need for piecing and matching the plaid strips. The yardage given allows for the inner border strips to be cut on the crosswise grain. Diagonally piece the strips as needed, referring to Diagonal Piecing instructions on page 118. Read through Border instructions on page 118 for general instructions on adding borders.

Cutting

From **BLACK PRINT**:
* Cut 3, 1-1/2 x 42-inch inner border strips

From **BLACK/TAN PLAID**:
* Cut 2, 3-1/2 x 40-inch side outer border strips
* Cut 2, 3-1/2 x 28-inch top/ bottom outer border strips

Attaching the Borders

Step 1 Attach the 1-1/2-inch wide **BLACK PRINT** inner border strips.

Step 2 Attach the 3-1/2-inch wide **BLACK/TAN PLAID** outer border strips.

Putting It All Together

Trim the backing and batting so they are 4-inches larger than the quilt top. Refer to **Finishing the Quilt** on page 118 for complete instructions.

Binding

Cutting

From **BLACK/TAN PLAID**:

* Cut enough 2-3/4-inch wide **bias** strips to make a 150-inch long strip

Sew the binding to the quilt using a 3/8-inch seam allowance. This measurement will produce a 1/2-inch wide finished double binding. Refer to **Binding** and **Diagonal Piecing** on page 119 for complete instructions.

Log Cabin Pines
32 x 38-inches

Log Cabin Pines Placemat

15 x 19-inches

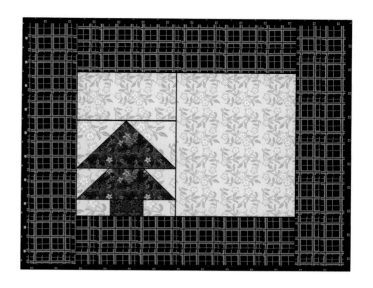

Fabrics and Supplies for one placemat

1/8 yard **GREEN PRINT** for tree block
1-1/2 x 2-1/2-inch piece **BROWN PRINT** for
    tree block
1/3 yard **WHEAT PRINT** for tree block and
    placemat top
1/4 yard **BLACK/TAN PLAID** for border
1/4 yard **BLACK PRINT** for binding
backing fabric, 19 x 23-inches
quilt batting, at least 19 x 23-inches

- Refer to **Log Cabin Pines** to cut and piece 1 tree block.

- From **WHEAT PRINT**:
    Cut 1, 9-1/2 x 10-1/2-inch rectangle
    Cut 1, 3-1/2 x 6-1/2-inch rectangle

- Sew the 3-1/2 x 6-1/2-inch rectangle to the top of the tree block; press. Sew the 9-1/2 x 10-1/2-inch rectangle to the right edge of the unit;press.

- From **BLACK/TAN PLAID**:
    Cut 2, 3-1/2 x 42-inch border strips

- Attach the 3-1/2-inch wide **BLACK/TAN PLAID** border strips. Read through **Border** instructions on page 118 for general instructions on adding borders.

- Trim the backing and batting so they are 4-inches larger than the placemat top. Refer to **Finishing the Quilt** on page 118 for complete instructions.

- From **BLACK PRINT**:
    Cut 2, 2-3/4 x 42-inch binding strips.

- Sew the binding to the quilt using a 3/8-inch seam allowance. This measurement will produce a 1/2-inch wide finished double binding. Refer to **Binding** and **Diagonal Piecing** on page 119 for complete instructions.

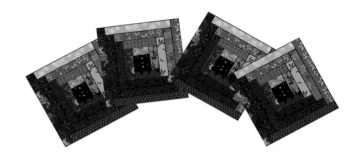

Log Cabin Pines Mug Mat

5-inches square

- Refer to **Log Cabin Pines** to make a Log Cabin block. Continue adding 1-inch wide strips until the block measures 5-1/2-inches square.

- Layer a 7-inch batting square, a 7-inch backing square, and the Log Cabin block, right sides together. Sew 1/4-inch from the Log Cabin block cut edges, leaving 3-inches open on one side.

- Trim the backing to 1/4-inch and trim the batting to the seam line. Turn the mug mat right side out, and press taking care to see that the corners are sharp and even.

- Hand stitch the opening closed.

Bear Paw

Bear Paw

28-inches square

Fabrics and Supplies

3/8 yard BEIGE PRINT for background

1/4 yard RED PRINT #1 for Bear Paw blocks

1/4 yard BLUE PRINT for Bear Paw blocks

1/2 yard GOLD FLORAL for center square, side and corner triangles

1/4 yard CHESTNUT PRINT for inner border

1/4 yard RED PRINT #2 for outer border

3/8 yard GOLD PLAID for binding (cut on the bias)

1 yard backing fabric

quilt batting, at least 32-inches square

Bear Paw Blocks

Make 4 blocks

Cutting

From **BEIGE PRINT**:
- Cut 3, 1-7/8 x 42-inch strips
- Cut 4, 1-1/2 x 42-inch strips.
   From the strips cut:
   24, 1-1/2 x 3-1/2-inch rectangles
   (8 of the rectangles will be used in the outer border)
   28, 1-1/2-inch squares

From **RED PRINT #1**:
- Cut 3, 1-7/8 x 42-inch strips
- Cut 1, 1-1/2 x 42-inch strip. From the strip cut:
   8, 1-1/2-inch squares. Set 4 of the squares aside to be used as corner squares for the inner border.

From **BLUE PRINT**:
- Cut 2, 2-1/2 x 42-inch strips.
   From the strips cut:
   28, 2-1/2-inch squares

Piecing

Step 1 With right sides together, layer the 1-7/8 x 42-inch **RED** and **BEIGE** strips together in pairs. Press together, but do not sew. Cut the layered strips into squares. Cut the layered squares in half diagonally to make 112 sets of triangles. Stitch 1/4-inch from the diagonal edge of each pair of triangles; press. <u>At this point each triangle-pieced square should measure 1-1/2-inches square.</u>

Crosscut 56, 1-7/8-inch squares

Make 112, 1-1/2-inch triangle-pieced squares

Step 2 Sew the triangle-pieced squares together in pairs; press.

Unit A
Make 28

Unit B
Make 28

Step 3 Sew a 1-1/2-inch **BEIGE** square to the right edge of each Unit B; press.

Unit B
Make 28

Step 4 Sew a Unit A to the right edge of a 2-1/2-inch **BLUE** square; press. Sew a Unit B to the bottom edge of the unit; press. <u>At this point the unit should measure 3-1/2-inches square.</u>

Unit A

Unit B

Make 28
Set 12 of the units aside to be used in the outer border

Step 5 Sew 2 of the Step 4 units to both side edges of a 1-1/2 x 3-1/2-inch **BEIGE** rectangle; press.

Make 8

Step 6 Sew a 1-1/2 x 3-1/2-inch **BEIGE** rectangle to both side edges of a 1-1/2 **RED #1** square; press.

Make 4

Step 7 Sew the Step 5 units to the top and bottom edges of the Step 6 units; press. <u>At this point each Bear Paw block should measure 7-1/2-inches square.</u>

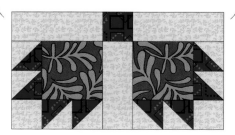

Make 4

Quilt Center

Cutting

From **GOLD FLORAL**:
* Cut 1, 12-1/2 x 42-inch strip.
  From this strip cut:
  1, 12-1/2-inch square. Cut the square diagonally into quarters to make 4 side triangles.
  Also cut 1, 7-1/2-inch center square
  Also cut 2, 7-inch squares. Cut the squares in half diagonally to make 4 corner triangles.

Side Triangles

Corner Triangles

Note: *The side and corner triangles are larger than necessary and will be trimmed before the borders are added.*

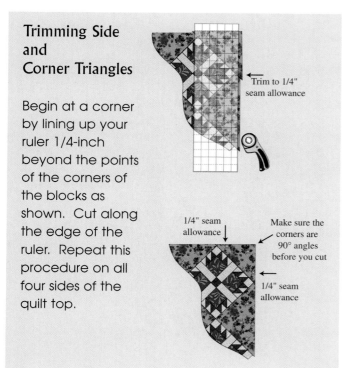

Trimming Side and Corner Triangles

Begin at a corner by lining up your ruler 1/4-inch beyond the points of the corners of the blocks as shown. Cut along the edge of the ruler. Repeat this procedure on all four sides of the quilt top.

Trim to 1/4" seam allowance

1/4" seam allowance

Make sure the corners are 90° angles before you cut

1/4" seam allowance

Quilt Center Assembly Diagram

Quilt Center Assembly

Step 1 Referring to the quilt center assembly diagram, lay out the Bear Paw blocks, center square, and side triangles in diagonal rows. Sew the pieces together. Press the seam allowances away from the Bear Paw blocks.

Step 2 Pin the rows together at the block intersections; sew together. Press the seam allowances in one direction. Add the corner triangles; press.

Step 3 Trim away the excess fabric from the side and corner triangles taking care to allow a 1/4-inch seam allowance beyond the corners of each block. Refer to **Trimming Side and Corner Triangles** for complete instructions.

Borders

Note: *The yardage given allows for the border strips to be cut on the crosswise grain. Diagonally piece the strips as needed, referring to* **Diagonal Piecing** *instructions on page 118. Read through* **Border** *instructions on page 118 for general instructions on adding borders.*

Cutting

From **CHESTNUT PRINT**:
- Cut 3, 1-1/2 x 42-inch inner border strips

From **RED PRINT #2**:
- Cut 2, 3-1/2 x 42-inch outer border strips

Note: *The 4, 1-1/2-inch RED #1 corner squares were cut previously in the Bear Paw block section. Also, the Bear Paw units were made previously.*

Attaching the Borders

Step 1 Attach the 1-1/2-inch wide **CHESTNUT** top/bottom inner border strips.

Step 2 For the side borders, measure the quilt from top to bottom including the seam allowances, but not the borders just added. Cut the 1-1/2-inch wide **CHESTNUT** side borders to this length. Sew a 1-1/2-inch **RED #1** square to each end of these border strips; press. Sew the borders to the quilt center; press.

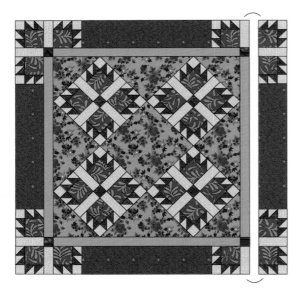

Step 3 For the top/bottom outer borders, measure the quilt center from side to side, including the borders just added. Subtract 8-inches from this measurement to allow for the Bear Paw units and the 1-1/2 x 3-1/2-inch **BEIGE** rectangles. Cut 2 of the 3-1/2-inch wide **RED #2** outer border strips to this length. Sew the Bear Paw units and the **BEIGE** rectangles to both ends of the the **RED #2** border strips. Sew the outer border strips to the quilt center; press.

Step 4 For the side outer borders, measure the quilt center from top to bottom, including the borders just added. Subtract 14-inches from this measurement to allow for the 2 Bear Paw units and the 1-1/2 x 3-1/2-inch **BEIGE** rectangles. Cut 2 of the 3-1/2-inch wide **RED #2** outer border strips to this length. Sew the **BEIGE** rectangles and the Bear Paw units to both ends of the the **RED #2** border strips. Sew the outer border strips to the quilt center; press.

Putting It All Together

Step 1 Trim the backing and batting so they are 4-inches larger than the quilt top. Mark the quilt top for quilting. Layer the backing, batting, and quilt top. Baste the 3 layers together and quilt as desired.

Step 2 To maintain perfect triangle tips at the outer edges, refer to the diagram. When trimming away the excess batting and backing after quilting, be sure to allow a 3/8-inch seam allowance beyond the points of the triangle tips. By taking a slightly wider seam allowance, you are able to maintain the points. The extra batting and backing will help fill the binding area.

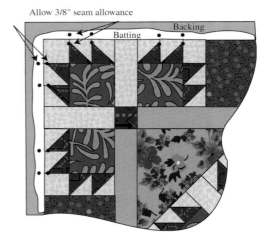

Allow 3/8" seam allowance
Backing
Batting

Step 3 Refer to **Finishing the Quilt** on page 118 for complete instructions.

Binding

Cutting

From **GOLD PLAID:**
- Cut enough 2-3/4-inch wide **bias** strips to make a 120-inch long strip

Sew the binding to the quilt using a 3/8-inch seam allowance. This measurement will produce a 1/2-inch wide finished double binding. Refer to **Binding** and **Diagonal Piecing** on page 119 for complete instructions.

Bear Paw
28-inches square

Pansy Square

64

Pansy Square

27-inches square

FABRICS AND SUPPLIES

1/3 yard BEIGE PRINT for applique foundation squares and lattice

1/8 yard RED FLORAL for flower appliques

1/8 yard RED PRINT for flower appliques, center square,
and corner posts

1/4 yard GREEN PRINT for leaf appliques and lattice

1/3 yard GOLD PRINT for flower center appliques and inner border

7/8 yard GREEN PLAID for outer border
(cut on the lengthwise grain)

1/3 yard RED PRINT for binding

7/8 yard backing fabric

quilt batting, at least 31-inches square

paper-backed fusible web

tear-away fabric stabilizer for applique (optional)

pearl cotton or machine-embroidery thread for decorative stitches:
gold and red

Quilt Center

Cutting

From **BEIGE PRINT**:
- Cut 1, 7-1/2 x 42-inch strip. From the strip cut:
  4, 7-1/2-inch squares

Applique - Fusible Web Method

Step 1 Position the fusible web, paper side up, over the applique shapes on page 68. With a pencil, trace 4 of petals #1, #2, #3, #4, and #5, 4 of the flower center, and 12 of the leaf, leaving a small margin between each shape. Cut the shapes apart.

Note: When you are fusing a large shape, like the leaf, fuse just the outer edges of the shape so that it will not look stiff when finished. To do this, draw a line about 3/8-inch inside the leaf, and cut away the fusible web on this line.

Step 2 Following the manufacturer's instructions, fuse the shapes to the wrong side of the fabric chosen for the appliques. Let the fabric cool and cut along the traced line. Peel away the paper backing from the fusible web.

Step 3 Referring to the block diagram on page 68, position the shapes on the 7-1/2-inch **BEIGE** squares; fuse in place.

Step 4 We machine buttonhole-stitched around the shapes using gold and red Mettler® embroidery thread for the top thread and regular sewing thread in the bobbin. If you like, you could hand buttonhole-stitch around the shapes with pearl cotton.

Buttonhole Stitch

Note: We suggest pinning a rectangle of tear-away stabilizer to the backside of the block to be appliqued so that it will lay flat when the applique is complete. We use the extra-light-weight Easy Tear™ sheets as a stabilizer. When the applique is complete, tear away the stabilizer.

Borders

*Note: The yardage given allows for the lattice strips and **GOLD** inner border strips to be cut on the crosswise grain. The yardage given allows for the **GREEN PLAID** outer border strips to be cut on the lengthwise grain (a couple extra inches are allowed for trimming). Read through **Border** instructions on page 118 for general instructions on adding borders.*

Cutting

From **GOLD PRINT**:
- Cut 2, 2 x 42-inch inner border strips

From **GREEN PRINT**:
- Cut 2, 1 x 42-inch strips

From **BEIGE PRINT**:
- Cut 1, 1 x 42-inch strip

From **RED PRINT**:
- Cut 5, 2-inch squares for center square and corner posts

From **GREEN PLAID**
(cut on the lengthwise grain):
- Cut 2, 5 x 31-inch side outer border strips
- Cut 2, 5 x 21-inch top/bottom outer border strips

Quilt Center and Attaching the Borders

Step 1 Aligning long edges, sew 1 x 42-inch **GREEN** strips to both side edges of the 1 x 42-inch **BEIGE** strip; press. Cut the strip set into segments.

Crosscut 4, 7-1/2-inch long lattice strips

Step 2 Sew appliqued flower blocks to both sides of a pieced lattice strip; press. Make 2 block rows. Sew 2 pieced lattice strips to both sides of the 2-inch **RED** center square; press. Sew the block rows to both sides of the lattice strip; press.

Step 3 Attach the 2-inch wide **GOLD** top/ bottom inner border strips.

Step 4 For the side borders, measure the quilt from top to bottom including the seam allowances, but not the borders just added. Cut the 2-inch wide **GOLD** border strips to this length. Sew a 2-inch **RED** corner square to the ends of both border strips; press. Sew the borders to the side edges of the quilt center; press.

Step 5 Attach the 5-inch wide **GREEN PLAID** outer border strips.

Putting It All Together

Trim the backing and batting so they are 4-inches larger than the quilt top. Refer to **Finishing the Quilt** on page 118 for complete instructions.

Binding

Cutting

From **RED PRINT**:
* Cut 3, 2-3/4 x 42-inch strips

Sew the binding to the quilt using a 3/8-inch seam allowance. This measurement will produce a 1/2-inch wide finished double binding. Refer to **Binding** and **Diagonal Piecing** on page 119 for complete instructions.

Pansy Square
27-inches square

Petal #3

Trace 4 onto fusible web

Petal #2

Petal #4

Petal #1

Petal #3

Petal #5

The applique shapes are reversed for tracing purposes.
When the applique is finished it will appear
as in the photograph.

Petal #1
Trace 4 onto fusible web

Petal #4

Trace 4 onto
fusible web

Flower Center
Trace 4
onto
fusible web

Petal #2
Trace 4 onto
fusible web

Petal #5

Trace 4 onto
fusible web

Leaf

Trace 12 onto
fusible web

Pansy Square Pillow

It is so easy to transform the Pansy Square wall quilt into a colorful pillow. This is a wonderful springtime pillow to add a cozy feeling to your adirondack chair. By cutting the outer border strips a little narrower, you will have the perfect size for a 24-inch pillow. The pillow is bound as you would a small quilt. We used wide binding as a decorative touch which is much easier than inserting a thick, covered cording at the pillow's edge.

Size: 24-inches square

Additional Fabrics and Supplies needed:

1-1/2 yards GREEN PRINT for pillow back
5/8 yard RED PRINT for binding
24-inch pillow form

Assemble the Pillow
- Make the Pansy Square wall quilt cutting 3-1/4-inch wide GREEN PRINT outer border strips.

- Quilt the pillow top as desired.

- From GREEN PRINT pillow back fabric:
    Cut 2, 24-1/2 x 30-inch rectangles

- With wrong sides together, fold the 2, 24-1/2 x 30-inch rectangles in half to make 2 double-thick 15 x 24-1/2-inch pillow back pieces. Overlap the folded edges by about 6-inches so that the pillow back measures 24-1/2-inches square. Stitch around the entire piece to create a single pillow back. The double thickness makes the pillow back more stable and finishes it nicely.

- With wrong sides together, layer the pillow top and pillow back; baste together.

- From RED PRINT binding fabric:
    Cut 3, 6-1/4 x 42-inch strips

- Sew the binding to the pillow using a 7/8-inch seam allowance. This measurement will produce a 7/8-inch wide finished double binding. Refer to Binding and Diagonal Piecing on page 119 for complete instructions.

- Insert the pillow form through the back opening.

Reindeer Trail

Reindeer Trail

26 x 28-inches

FABRICS AND SUPPLIES

1/8 yard GOLD PRINT #1 for star blocks and flower blocks

1/8 yard GOLD PRINT #2 for star blocks and star appliques

1/8 yard GOLD PRINT #3 for star blocks and lattice strips

1/8 yard BEIGE PRINT #1 for star blocks and applique foundation

1/4 yard BEIGE PRINT #2 for star blocks, applique foundation,
and flower blocks

1/8 yard RED PRINT #1 for flower blocks

1/8 yard GREEN PRINT #1 for flower blocks

1/8 yard GREEN PRINT #2 for flower blocks and tree applique

1/8 yard RED PRINT #2 for lattice strips

1/8 yard BLACK PRINT for lattice posts and corner squares

1/8 yard RED PRINT #3 for triangle blocks

1/8 yard GREEN PRINT #3 for triangle blocks

1/4 yard BEIGE PRINT #3 for triangle blocks

1/8 yard BROWN PRINT for deer applique

1/2 yard RED PRINT #4 for outer border

1/3 yard BLACK PRINT for binding

7/8 yard backing fabric

quilt batting, at least 30 x 32-inches

paper-backed fusible web

pearl cotton or machine-embroidery thread
for decorative stitches: black

Star Block Unit

Cutting

From **GOLD PRINT #1**:
- Cut 1, 7/8 x 42-inch strip

From **GOLD PRINT #2**:
- Cut 1, 7/8 x 42-inch strip

From **GOLD PRINT #3**:
- Cut 1, 1-1/2 x 42-inch strip. From the strip cut:
  - 24, 1-1/2-inch squares
  - 3, 1-inch squares for center squares

From **BEIGE PRINT #1**:
- Cut 1, 1-1/2 x 42-inch strip. From the strip cut:
  - 8, 1-1/2 x 2-1/2-inch rectangles
  - 8, 1-1/2-inch squares

From **BEIGE PRINT #2**:
- Cut 1, 1-1/2 x 20-inch strip. From the strip cut:
  - 4, 1-1/2 x 2-1/2-inch rectangles
  - 4, 1-1/2-inch squares

Piecing

Step 1 Sew a 7/8-inch wide **GOLD PRINT #1** strip to a 1-inch **GOLD PRINT #3** square. Press the seam allowance toward the strip, and trim the strip even with the edges of the square.

Step 2 Turn the unit to the left a quarter turn and sew a 7/8-inch wide **GOLD PRINT #1** strip to the unit; press and trim.

Step 3 Turn the unit to the left a quarter turn and sew a 7/8-inch wide **GOLD PRINT #1** strip to the unit; press and trim.

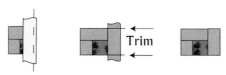

Step 4 Turn the unit to the left a quarter turn and sew another 7/8-inch wide **GOLD PRINT #1** strip to the unit; press and trim.

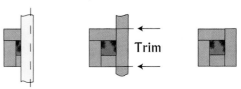

Step 5 Continue this process adding the 7/8-inch wide **GOLD PRINT #2** strips, referring to the log cabin unit diagram for color placement. Press and trim each strip before adding the next. After adding a total of 2 strips to each side of the **GOLD** center square, the log cabin unit should measure 2-1/2-inches square.

Log Cabin Unit
Make 3

Step 6 Position a 1-1/2-inch **GOLD PRINT #3** square on the corner of a 1-1/2 x 2-1/2-inch **BEIGE PRINT #1** rectangle. Draw a diagonal line on the square, and stitch on the line. Trim the seam allowance to 1/4-inch, and press. Repeat this process at the opposite corner of the rectangle.

Make 8
star point units

Step 7 Sew Step 6 star point units to the top and bottom edges of a log cabin unit; press. Sew 1-1/2-inch **BEIGE PRINT #1** squares to both ends of the remaining star point units; press. Sew the star point units to both side edges of the log cabin unit; press. At this point each star block should measure 4-1/2-inches square.

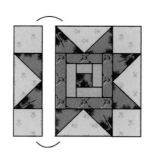

Make 2

Step 8 Repeat Steps 6 and 7 using 1-1/2-inch **GOLD PRINT #3** squares, 1-1/2 x 2-1/2-inch **BEIGE PRINT #2** rectangles, and 1-1/2-inch **BEIGE PRINT #2** squares.

Make 4
star point units

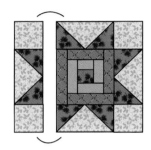

Make 1

Step 9 Sew the star blocks together; press. <u>At this point the star unit should measure 4-1/2 x 12-1/2-inches</u>.

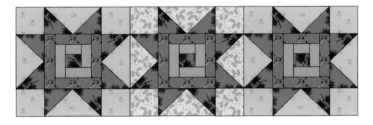

Make 1

Reindeer and Tree Foundation Section

Cutting

From **BEIGE PRINT #1**:
• Cut 1, 1-1/2 x 42-inch strip

From **BEIGE PRINT #2**:
• Cut 1, 1-1/2 x 42-inch strip

Piecing

Step 1 Aligning long edges sew the 1-1/2 x 42-inch **BEIGE PRINT #1** and **BEIGE PRINT #2** strips together. Press, referring to **Pressing Strip Sets** on page 114. Cut the strip set into segments.

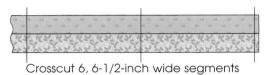

Crosscut 6, 6-1/2-inch wide segments

Step 2 Sew 3 segments together to complete the foundation for the applique; press. <u>At this point each pieced foundation square should measure 6-1/2-inches square</u>.

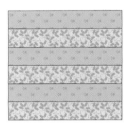

Make 2

Step 3 Referring to the quilt diagram, sew the pieced foundation squares together; press.

Flower Section

Cutting

From **GOLD PRINT #1**:
• Cut 1, 1-1/2 x 8-inch strip

From **RED PRINT #1**:
• Cut 1, 1-1/2 x 20-inch strip. From the strip cut:
    1, 1-1/2 x 8-inch strip
    4, 1-1/2 x 2-1/2-inch rectangles

From **GREEN PRINT #1**:
• Cut 1, 1-1/2 x 22-inch strip. From the strip cut:
    8, 1-1/2 x 2-1/2-inch rectangles

From **GREEN PRINT #2**:
• Cut 1, 1-1/2 x 8-inch strip. From the strip cut:
    4, 1-1/2-inch squares

From **BEIGE PRINT #2**:
• Cut 1, 1-1/2 x 15-inch strip. From the strip cut:
    8, 1-1/2-inch squares

Piecing

Step 1 Aligning long edges, sew the 1-1/2 x 8-inch **GOLD PRINT #1** and **RED PRINT #1** strips together; press. Cut the strip set into segments.

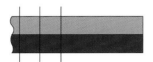

Crosscut 4, 1-1/2-inch wide segments

Step 2 Sew a 1-1/2 x 2-1/2-inch **RED PRINT #1** rectangle to the side edge of each Step 1 unit; press.

Make 4

Step 3 Position a 1-1/2-inch **BEIGE** square on the left corner of a 1-1/2 x 2-1/2-inch **GREEN PRINT #1** rectangle. Referring to the diagram, draw a diagonal line on the square; stitch on the line. Trim the seam allowance to 1/4-inch; press.

Leaf A
Make 4

Leaf B
Make 4

Step 4 Sew a Leaf A to the right edge of a Step 2 unit; press. Add a 1-1/2-inch **GREEN PRINT #2** square to the right edge of a Leaf B; press. Sew this unit to the bottom edge of a flower unit; and press. <u>At this point each flower block should measure 3-1/2-inches square</u>.

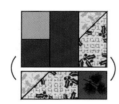

( ) Make 4

Step 5 Sew the 4 flower blocks together; press. <u>At this point the flower unit should measure 3-1/2 x 12-1/2-inches</u>.

Quilt Center

Cutting

From **RED PRINT #2**:
- Cut 1, 1-1/2 x 42-inch strip.
  From the strip cut:
  2, 1-1/2 x 12-1/2-inch lattice strips
  2, 1-1/2 x 4-1/2-inch lattice strips

From **GOLD PRINT #3**:
- Cut 1, 1-1/2 x 42-inch strip.
  From the strip cut:
  1, 1-1/2 x 12-1/2-inch lattice strip
  2, 1-1/2 x 9-1/2-inch lattice strips

From **BLACK PRINT**:
- Cut 1, 1-1/2 x 11-inch strip.
  From the strip cut:
  6, 1-1/2-inch square lattice posts

Quilt Center Assembly

Step 1 Referring to the quilt diagram, sew a 1-1/2 x 12-1/2-inch **RED PRINT #2** lattice strip to the top/bottom edges of the star unit; press.

Step 2 Sew the flower unit to the bottom edge of the pieced foundation unit and sew to the bottom of the Step 1 unit; press.

Step 3 Sew the 1-1/2 x 12-1/2-inch **GOLD PRINT #3** lattice strip to the bottom edge of the Step 2 unit; press.

Step 4 To make the side lattice strips, sew together a 1-1/2 x 4-1/2-inch **RED PRINT #2** lattice strip, a 1-1/2 x 9-1/2-inch **GOLD PRINT #3** lattice strip, and 3, 1-1/2-inch **BLACK PRINT #1** lattice posts; press. Make 2 lattice strips. Sew the lattice strips to the side edges of the quilt center; press.

Applique - Fusible Web Method

Step 1 Position the fusible web, paper side up, over the applique shapes. With a pencil trace the shapes onto the fusible web the number of times indicated on the pattern pieces, leaving a small margin between each shape. Cut the shapes apart.

Step 2 Following the manufacturer's instructions, fuse the shapes to the wrong side of the fabrics chosen for the appliques. Let the fabric cool and cut along the traced line. Peel away the paper backing from the fusible web.

Step 3 Referring to the quilt diagram, position the applique shapes on the quilt center; fuse in place.

Note: We suggest pinning a rectangle of tear-away stabilizer to the backside of the block to be appliqued so that it will lay flat when the applique is complete. We use the extra-light-weight Easy Tear™ sheets as a stabilizer. When the applique is complete, tear away the stabilizer.

Step 4 We machine buttonhole-stitched around the shapes using Mettler® embroidery thread for the top thread and regular sewing thread in the bobbin. If you like, you could hand buttonhole-stitch around the shapes with pearl cotton.

Buttonhole Stitch

Note: To prevent the hand buttonhole-stitches from "rolling off" the edges of the applique shapes, take an extra backstitch in the same place as you made the buttonhole stitch, going around outer curves, corners, and points. For straight edges, taking a backstitch every inch is enough.

Hourglass Block Borders

Cutting

From **RED PRINT #3**:
- Cut 1, 3-1/4 x 42-inch strip.
  From the strip cut:
  7, 3-1/4-inch squares. Cut the squares diagonally into quarters, forming 28 triangles.

From **GREEN PRINT #3**:
- Cut 1, 3-1/4 x 42-inch strip.
  From the strip cut:
  8, 3-1/4-inch squares. Cut the squares diagonally into quarters, forming 32 triangles.

From **BEIGE PRINT #3**:
- Cut 2, 3-1/4 x 42-inch strips.
  From the strips cut:
  15, 3-1/4-inch squares. Cut the squares diagonally into quarters, forming 60 triangles.

From **BLACK PRINT**:
- Cut 4, 2-1/2-inch corner squares

Piecing

Step 1 Layer a **BEIGE** triangle on a **RED** triangle. Stitch along the bias edge as shown; press. Repeat with the remaining 27 **RED** triangles and 27 **BEIGE** triangles. Make sure you position the **BEIGE** triangle on top, and sew along the same bias edge of each triangle set so that your pieced triangle units will all have the **BEIGE** triangles on the same side.

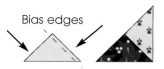

Make 28 triangle units

Step 2 Sew the Step 1 triangle units together in pairs; press. <u>At this point each hourglass block should measure 2-1/2-inches square.</u>

Make 14

Step 3 Repeat Step 1 layering the remaining 32 **BEIGE** triangles on the 32 **GREEN** triangles.

Bias edges

Make 32 triangle units

Step 4 Sew the Step 3 triangle units together in pairs; press. <u>At this point each hourglass block should measure 2-1/2-inches square.</u>

Make 16

Step 5 For the top/bottom hourglass block borders, refer to the diagram and sew together 4 **GREEN/BEIGE** blocks and 3 **RED/BEIGE** blocks; press. Make 2 borders. <u>At this point each hourglass block border should measure 2-1/2 x 14-1/2-inches.</u> Sew the borders to the top/bottom edges of the quilt center; press.

Make 2

Step 6 For the side hourglass block borders, refer to the diagram and sew together 4 **GREEN/BEIGE** blocks and 4 **RED/ BEIGE** blocks; press. Make 2 borders. Sew 2-1/2-inch **BLACK** corner squares to the ends of both of the borders; press. <u>At this point each hourglass block border should measure 2-1/2 x 20-1/2-inches.</u> Referring to the quilt diagram for placement, sew the borders to the sides of the quilt center; press.

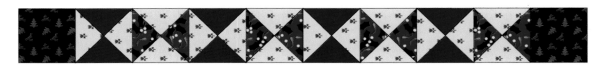

Make 2

Border

Note: *The yardage given allows for the border strips to be cut on the crosswise grain. Read through **Border** instructions on page 118 for general instructions on adding borders.*

Cutting

From **RED PRINT #4**:
• Cut 3, 4-1/2 x 42-inch border strips

Attaching the Border

Attach the 4-1/2-inch wide **RED PRINT #4** border strips.

Putting It All Together

Trim the backing and backing so they are 4-inches larger than the quilt top. Refer to **Finishing the Quilt** on page 118 for complete instructions.

Binding

Cutting

From **BLACK PRINT**:
• Cut 3, 2-3/4 x 42-inch strips

Sew the binding to the quilt using a 3/8-inch seam allowance. This measurement will produce a 1/2-inch wide finished double binding. Refer to **Binding** and **Diagonal Piecing** on page 119 for complete instructions.

Reindeer Trail
26 x 28-inches

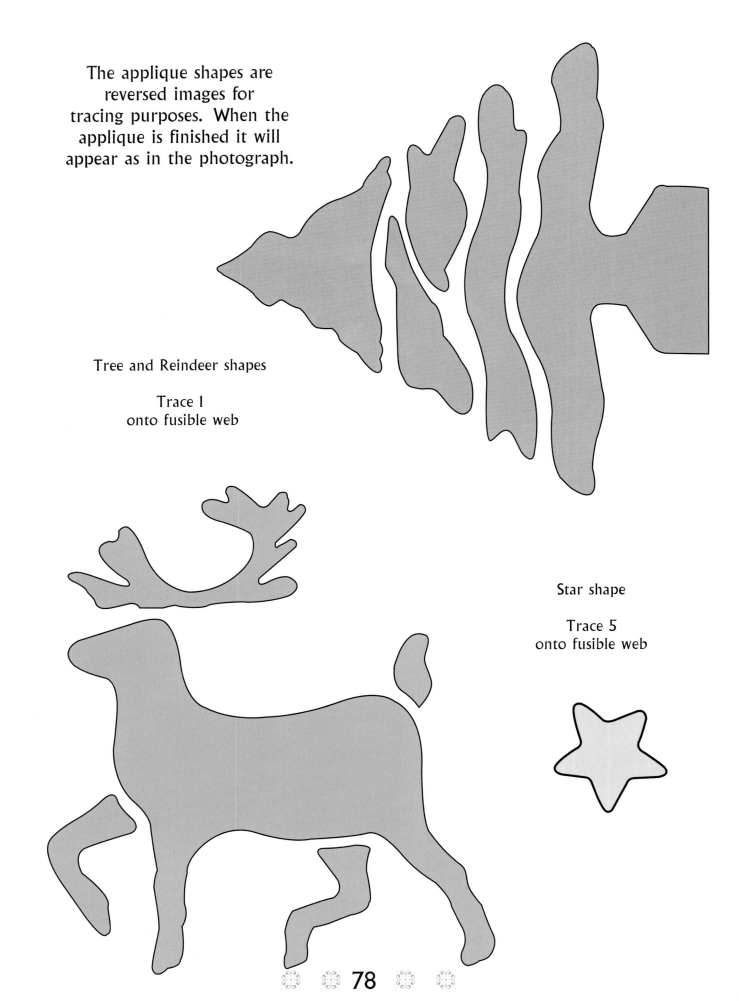

The applique shapes are reversed images for tracing purposes. When the applique is finished it will appear as in the photograph.

Tree and Reindeer shapes

Trace 1
onto fusible web

Star shape

Trace 5
onto fusible web

Jack-o-Lantern Trail

Transform the Reindeer Trail pattern into a tribute to autumn. Using whimsical jack-o-lantern applique shapes and colorful autumn fabrics - ranging from toasty brown to deep shades of goldenrod - create a fall seasonal backdrop.

Prepare the jack-o-lantern applique shapes referring to Applique-Fusible Web Method on page 75.

Jack-o-Lantern Trail
26 x 28-inches

The applique shapes are reversed images for tracing purposes. When the applique is finished it will appear as in the photograph.

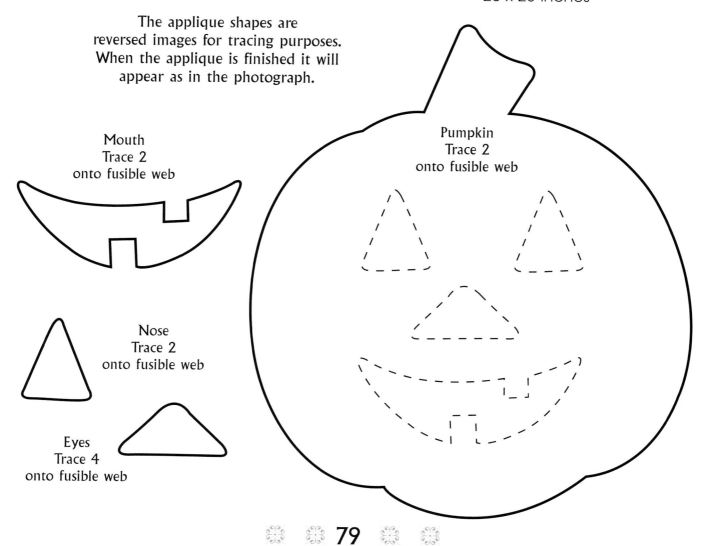

Mouth
Trace 2
onto fusible web

Pumpkin
Trace 2
onto fusible web

Nose
Trace 2
onto fusible web

Eyes
Trace 4
onto fusible web

Snow & Treats

21-inches square

FABRICS AND SUPPLIES

1/3 yard MEDIUM BLUE PRINT for applique foundation squares
and star blocks

1/4 yard BEIGE PRINT for snowman appliques and checkerboard border

1/8 yard GOLD PRINT for center star and star blocks

1/4 yard RED PRINT for lattice and pieced border

1/3 yard DARK BLUE PRINT for checkerboard border and outer border

1/3 yard RED PRINT for binding

3/4 yard backing fabric

quilt batting, at least 25-inches square

paper-backed fusible web

tear-away fabric stabilizer for applique (optional)

pearl cotton or machine-embroidery thread for decorative stitches: black

Quilt Center

Cutting

From **MEDIUM BLUE PRINT**:
- Cut 1, 4-1/2 x 20-inch strip. From the strip cut:
  4, 4-1/2-inch squares

From **GOLD PRINT**:
- Cut 1, 1-1/2 x 42-inch strip. From the strip cut:
  5, 1-1/2 x 3-1/2-inch rectangles
  10, 1-1/2-inch squares

From **RED PRINT**:
- Cut 1, 1-1/2 x 42-inch strip. From the strip cut:
  4, 1-1/2 x 4-1/2-inch rectangles

Applique - Fusible Web Method

Step 1 Position the fusible web, paper side up, over the applique shape. With a pencil, trace the shape onto fusible web the number of times indicated on the pattern pieces, leaving a small margin between each shape. Cut the shapes apart.

Note: *When you are fusing a large shape, like the snowman, fuse just the outer edges of the shape so that it will not look stiff when finished. To do this, draw a line about 3/8-inch inside the snowman, and cut away the fusible web on this line.*

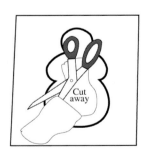

Step 2 Following the manufacturer's instructions, fuse the shapes to the wrong side of the fabric chosen for the appliques. Let the fabric cool and cut along the traced line. Peel away the paper backing from the fusible web.

Step 3 Referring to the block diagram, position the shapes on the 4-1/2-inch **MEDIUM BLUE** squares; fuse in place.

Note: *We suggest pinning a rectangle of tear-away stabilizer to the backside of the block to be appliqued so that it will lay flat when the applique is complete. We use the extra-light-weight Easy Tear™ sheets as a stabilizer. When the applique is complete, tear away the stabilizer.*

Step 4 We machine buttonhole-stitched around the shapes using black Mettler® embroidery thread for the top thread and regular sewing thread in the bobbin. If you like, you could hand buttonhole-stitch around the shapes with pearl cotton. The eyes and buttons were made with French knots, the arms were made with the stem/outline stitch, and the mouths were made with the straight stitch.

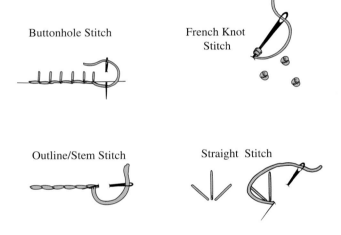

Buttonhole Stitch

French Knot Stitch

Outline/Stem Stitch

Straight Stitch

Step 5 Position a 1-1/2-inch **GOLD** square on the corner of a 1-1/2 x 4-1/2-inch **RED** rectangle. Draw a diagonal line on the square and stitch on the line. Trim the seam allowance to 1/4-inch; press. Refer to the quilt diagram for placement and sew the appliqued blocks to the side edges of both of the lattice strips; press. <u>At this point each block row should measure 4-1/2 x 9-1/2-inches</u>. (The remaining **GOLD** squares will be used for the star blocks.)

Make 2 lattice strips

Step 6 Position a 1-1/2 x 3-1/2-inch **GOLD** rectangle on the right corner of a 1-1/2 x 4-1/2-inch **RED** rectangle. Draw a diagonal line on the rectangle, stitch, trim; press. Position a 1-1/2 x 4-1/2-inch **RED** rectangle on the right corner of the unit. Draw a diagonal line on the rectangle, stitch, trim; press. <u>At this point the lattice strip should measure 1-1/2 x 9-1/2-inches.</u> (The remaining **GOLD** rectangles will be used for the star blocks.)

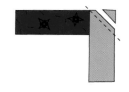

Make 1

Step 7 Sew the Step 5 block rows to the top/bottom edges of the Step 6 lattice strip; press. <u>At this point the quilt center should measure 9-1/2-inches square.</u>

Borders

Note: The yardage given allows for the border strips to be cut on the crosswise grain. Read through **Border** instructions on page 118 for general instructions on adding borders.

Cutting

From **DARK BLUE PRINT**:
- Cut 2, 3-1/2 x 42-inch outer border strips
- Cut 1, 1-1/2 x 42-inch strip

From **BEIGE PRINT**:
- Cut 1, 1-1/2 x 42-inch strip

From **RED PRINT**:
- Cut 2, 1-1/2 x 42-inch strips.
  From the strips cut:
      8, 1-1/2 x 9-1/2-inch strips

From **MEDIUM BLUE PRINT**:
- Cut 2, 1-1/2 x 42-inch strips.

From the strips cut:
    8, 1-1/2 x 2-1/2-inch rectangles
    16, 1-1/2-inch squares

Note: The **GOLD PRINT** squares and rectangles were cut earlier.

Assembling and Attaching the Borders

Step 1 Aligning long edges, sew together the **BEIGE** and **DARK BLUE** 1-1/2 x 42-inch strips; press. Cut the strip set into segments.

Crosscut 20, 1-1/2-inch wide segments

Step 2 Sew together 5 of the Step 1 segments; press. Make 4 checkerboard strips. Remove a 1-1/2-inch **BEIGE** square from the end of each checkerboard strip. <u>At this point each strip should measure 1-1/2 x 9-1/2-inches.</u>

Make 4

Step 3 Sew a **RED** 1-1/2 x 9-1/2-inch strip to the top/bottom edges of each checkerboard strip; press. Sew 2 of the pieced borders to the top/bottom edges of the quilt center; press.

Step 4 Position a 1-1/2-inch **GOLD** square on the right corner of a 1-1/2 x 2-1/2-inch **MEDIUM BLUE** rectangle. Draw a diagonal line on the square, stitch, trim; press. Sew a 1-1/2-inch **MEDIUM BLUE** square to the right edge of the unit; press. <u>At this point each unit should measure 1-1/2 x 3-1/2-inches.</u>

  Make 8

Step 5 Position 1-1/2-inch **MEDIUM BLUE** squares on the corners of a 1-1/2 x 3-1/2-inch **GOLD** rectangle. Draw a diagonal line on the squares, stitch, trim; press. <u>At this point each unit should measure 1-1/2 x 3-1/2-inches.</u>

   Make 4

Step 6 Sew the Step 4 units to the top/bottom edges of the Step 5 units; press. <u>At this point each star block should measure 3-1/2-inches square.</u> Make 4 star blocks. Sew the star blocks to both ends of the remaining pieced border strips; press. Sew the pieced borders to the side edges of the quilt center; press.

  Make 4

Step 7 Attach the 3-1/2-inch wide **DARK BLUE** outer border strips.

Putting It All Together

Trim the backing and batting so they are 4-inches larger than the quilt top. Refer to **Finishing the Quilt** on page 118 for complete instructions.

Binding

Cutting

From **RED PRINT**:
- Cut 3, 2-3/4 x 42-inch strips

Sew the binding to the quilt using a 3/8-inch seam allowance. This measurement will produce a 1/2-inch wide finished double binding. Refer to **Binding** and **Diagonal Piecing** on page 119 for complete instructions.

Placement Diagram

Snow Treats
21-inches square

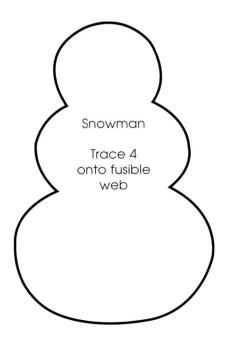

Snowman

Trace 4
onto fusible
web

Sunflower Glory

Sunflower & Glory

15-inches square

FABRICS AND SUPPLIES

3/8 yard BEIGE PRINT for sawtooth and middle borders

1/8 yard GREEN PRINT for leaf appliques and large corner posts

1/8 yard GOLD PRINT for flower applique and small corner posts

1/8 yard BLACK PRINT for flower center applique and sawtooth borders

1/4 yard GOLD ACORN PRINT for outer border

1/4 yard BLACK PRINT for binding

1/2 yard backing fabric

quilt batting, at least 19-inches square

paper-backed fusible web

tear-away fabric stabilizer for applique (optional)

pearl cotton or machine-embroidery thread for decorative stitches: black

Quilt Center

Cutting

From **BEIGE PRINT**:
- Cut 1, 5-1/2-inch square

Applique - Fusible Web Method

Step 1 Position the fusible web, paper side up, over the applique shapes. With a pencil, trace the shapes onto fusible web the number of times indicated on the pattern pieces, leaving a small margin between each shape. Cut the shapes apart.

Note: *When you are fusing a large shape, like the leaves, fuse just the outer edges of the shape so that it will not look stiff when finished. To do this, draw a line about 3/8-inch inside the leaf, and cut away the fusible web on this line.*

Step 2 Following the manufacturer's instructions, fuse the shapes to the wrong side of the fabric chosen for the appliques. Let the fabric cool and cut along the traced line. Peel away the paper backing from the fusible web.

Step 3 Referring to the placement diagram, trace the placement circles onto the 5-1/2-inch **BEIGE** square. Position the prepared leaf shapes along the leaf edge placement line; fuse in place.

Step 4 Position 4 of the prepared flower petal shapes atop the leaves and along the petal edge placement line; fuse in place. Position the remaining flower petal shapes between the petals and along the petal edge placement line; fuse in place. Position the prepared flower center on the flower unit so the bottom edges of flower petals are covered; fuse in place.

Note: *We suggest pinning a rectangle of tear-away stabilizer to the backside of the block to be appliqued so that it will lay flat when the applique is complete. We use the extra-light-weight Easy Tear™ sheets as a stabilizer. When the applique is complete, tear away the stabilizer.*

Step 5 We machine buttonhole-stitched around the shapes using black Mettler® embroidery thread for the top thread and regular sewing thread in the bobbin. If you like, you could hand buttonhole-stitch around the shapes with pearl cotton.

Buttonhole Stitch

Sawtooth Borders

Cutting

From **BEIGE PRINT**:
- Cut 2, 1-7/8 x 42-inch strips

From **BLACK PRINT**:
- Cut 2, 1-7/8 x 42-inch strips

Piecing

Step 1 With right sides together, layer the 1-7/8 x 42-inch **BEIGE** and **BLACK** strips together in pairs. Press together, but do not sew. Cut the layered strips into squares. Cut the layered squares in half diagonally to make 56 sets of triangles. Stitch 1/4-inch from the diagonal edge of each pair of triangles; press. <u>At this point each triangle-pieced square should measure 1-1/2-inches square</u>.

Crosscut 28,
1-7/8-inch squares

Make 56, 1-1/2-inch
triangle-pieced squares

Step 2 For the inner sawtooth borders sew together 5 triangle-pieced squares; press. <u>At this point each sawtooth border strip should measure 1-1/2 x 5-1/2-inches</u>.

Make 4

Step 3 For the outer sawtooth borders sew together 9 triangle-pieced squares; press. <u>At this point each sawtooth border strip should measure 1-1/2 x 9-1/2-inches.</u>

Make 4

Borders

Note: *The yardage given allows for the border strips to be cut on the crosswise grain. Read through* **Border** *instructions on page 118 for general instructions on adding borders.*

Cutting

From **BEIGE PRINT**:
- Cut 2, 1-1/2 x 42-inch strips.
   From the strips cut:
      8, 1-1/2-inch squares. The remaining strips will be used for the middle border.

From **GOLD PRINT**:
- Cut 4, 1-1/2-inch corner post squares

From **GOLD ACORN PRINT**:
- Cut 2, 2-1/2 x 42-inch outer border strips

From **GREEN PRINT**:
- Cut 4, 2-1/2-inch corner post squares

Attaching the Borders

Step 1 Sew inner sawtooth border strips to the top/bottom edges of the appliqued **BEIGE** square; press. Sew 1-1/2-inch **BEIGE** squares to both edges of the remaining inner sawtooth border strips; press. Sew the border strips to the side edges of the appliqued **BEIGE** square; press. <u>At this point the quilt center should measure 7-1/2-inches square.</u>

Step 2 Attach the 1-1/2-inch wide **BEIGE** top/bottom middle border strips.

Step 3 For the side middle borders, measure the quilt from top to bottom through the middle, including the seam allowances, but not the top/bottom borders. Cut 2, 1-1/2-inch wide **BEIGE** side middle border strips to this length. Sew a 1-1/2-inch **GOLD** corner post square to both ends of the border strips; press. Sew the border strips to the quilt center; press. <u>At this point the quilt center should measure 9-1/2-inches square.</u>

Step 4 Sew outer sawtooth border strips to the top/bottom edges of the quilt center; press. Sew 1-1/2-inch **BEIGE** squares to both ends of the remaining outer sawtooth border strips; press. Sew the border strips to the side edges of the quilt center; press. <u>At this point the quilt center should measure 11-1/2-inches square.</u>

Step 5 Attach the 2-1/2-inch wide **GOLD ACORN PRINT** top/bottom outer border strips.

Step 6 For the side outer border strips, measure the quilt from top to bottom through the middle, including the seam allowances, but not the top/bottom borders. Cut 2, 2-1/2-inch wide **GOLD ACORN PRINT** outer border strips to this length. Sew a 2-1/2-inch **GREEN** corner post square to both ends of the border strips; press. Sew the border strips to the quilt center; press.

Putting It All Together

Trim the backing and batting so they are 4-inches larger than the quilt top. Refer to **Finishing the Quilt** on page 118 for complete instructions.

Binding

Cutting

From **BLACK PRINT**:
- Cut 2, 2-3/4 x 42-inch strips

Sew the binding to the quilt using a 3/8-inch seam allowance. This measurement will produce a 1/2-inch wide finished double binding. Refer to **Binding** and **Diagonal Piecing** on page 119 for complete instructions.

Sunflower Glory
15-inches square

Leaf Edge Placement

Petal Edge Placement

Placement Diagram

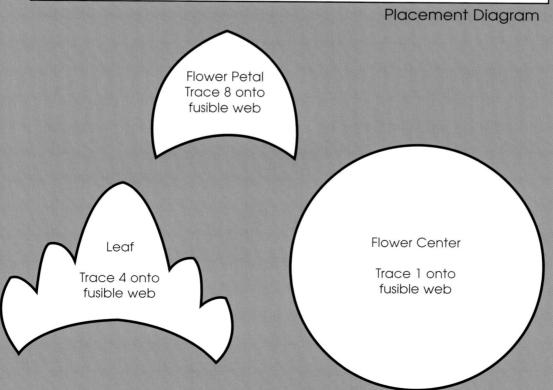

Flower Petal
Trace 8 onto
fusible web

Leaf

Trace 4 onto
fusible web

Flower Center

Trace 1 onto
fusible web

Table Topper Square

Table Topper Square

30-inches square

FABRICS AND SUPPLIES

1/4 yard LIGHT BLUE PRINT for blocks

3/8 yard LIGHT BEIGE PRINT for background

1/4 yard BEIGE PRINT for blocks

1/3 yard RED PRINT for inner border

1/2 yard BLUE FLORAL for outer border

3/8 yard RED PRINT for binding

1 yard backing fabric

quilt batting, at least 34-inches square

Broken Dishes Blocks

Make 5 **LIGHT BLUE/LIGHT BEIGE** blocks
Make 4 **BEIGE/LIGHT BEIGE** blocks

Cutting

From **LIGHT BLUE PRINT**:
• Cut 3, 2-3/8 x 42-inch strips

From **LIGHT BEIGE PRINT**:
• Cut 5, 2-3/8 x 42-inch strips

From **BEIGE PRINT**:
• Cut 2, 2-3/8 x 42-inch strips

Piecing

Step 1 With right sides together, layer together the 2-3/8 x 42-inch **LIGHT BLUE** strips and 3 of the **LIGHT BEIGE** strips in pairs. Press together, but do not sew. Cut the layered strips into squares. Cut the layered squares in half diagonally to make 80 sets of triangles. Stitch 1/4-inch from the diagonal edge of each set of triangles; press. <u>At this point each triangle-pieced square should measure 2-inches square.</u>

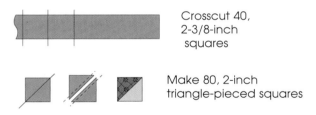

Crosscut 40, 2-3/8-inch squares

Make 80, 2-inch triangle-pieced squares

Step 2 Referring to the block diagram, sew the triangle-pieced squares together in 4 horizontal rows. Press the seam allowances in alternating directions by rows so the seams will fit snugly together with less bulk. Sew the rows together; press. <u>At this point each block should measure 6-1/2-inches square.</u>

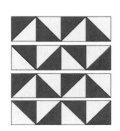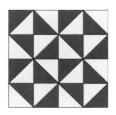

Make 5

Step 3 Repeat the process as in Steps 1 and 2 layering the 2-3/8 x 42-inch **BEIGE** strips and 2 of the **LIGHT BEIGE** strips in pairs. Make 64, 2-inch triangle-pieced squares.

Crosscut 32, 2-3/8-inch squares

Make 64, 2-inch triangle-pieced squares

Step 4 Referring to the block diagram, sew the units together in 4 horizontal rows. Press the seam allowances in alternating directions by rows so the seams will fit snugly together with less bulk. Sew the rows together; press. <u>At this point each block should measure 6-1/2-inches square.</u>

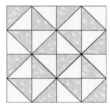

Make 4

Quilt Center & Borders

Note: *The yardage given allows for the border strips to be cut on the crosswise grain. Read through* **Border** *instructions on page 118 for general instructions on adding borders.*

Cutting

From **RED PRINT**:
• Cut 4, 2-1/2 x 42-inch strips.
  From the strips cut:
      2, 2-1/2 x 30-1/2-inch inner border strips
      2, 2-1/2 x 18-1/2-inch inner border strips
      4, 2-1/2 x 4-1/2-inch rectangles

From **BLUE FLORAL**:
• Cut 3, 4-1/2 x 42-inch strips.
  From the strips cut:
      4, 4-1/2 x 18-1/2-inch outer border strips
      4, 4-1/2-inch squares

Piecing

Step 1 Referring to the quilt diagram for block placement, sew the blocks together in 3 horizontal rows of 3 blocks each, alternating the blocks. Press the seam allowances in alternating directions by rows so the seams will fit snugly together with less bulk. <u>At this point the quilt center should measure 18-1/2-inches square</u>.

Step 2 Aligning long edges, sew together a 2-1/2 x 18-1/2-inch **RED** inner border strip and a 4-1/2 x 18-1/2-inch **BLUE FLORAL** outer border strip; press. Make 2 pieced borders. Sew the pieced borders to the top/bottom of the quilt; press.

Step 3 Attach the 2-1/2 x 30-1/2-inch **RED** inner border strips to the sides of the quilt; press.

Step 4 Sew the 2-1/2 x 4-1/2-inch **RED** rectangles to both sides of 2 of the 4-1/2 x 18-1/2-inch **BLUE FLORAL** strips. Add the 4-1/2-inch **BLUE FLORAL** squares to both ends of these strips; press. Sew the border strips to the sides of the quilt; press.

Putting It All Together

Trim the backing and batting so they are about 4-inches larger than the table topper. Refer to **Finishing the Quilt** on page 118 for complete instructions.

Binding

Cutting

From **RED PRINT**:
• Cut 4, 2-3/4 x 42-inch strips

Sew the binding to the table topper using a 3/8-inch seam allowance. This measurement will produce a 1/2-inch wide finished double binding. Refer to **Binding** and **Diagonal Piecing** on page 119 for complete instructions.

Table Topper Square
30-inches square

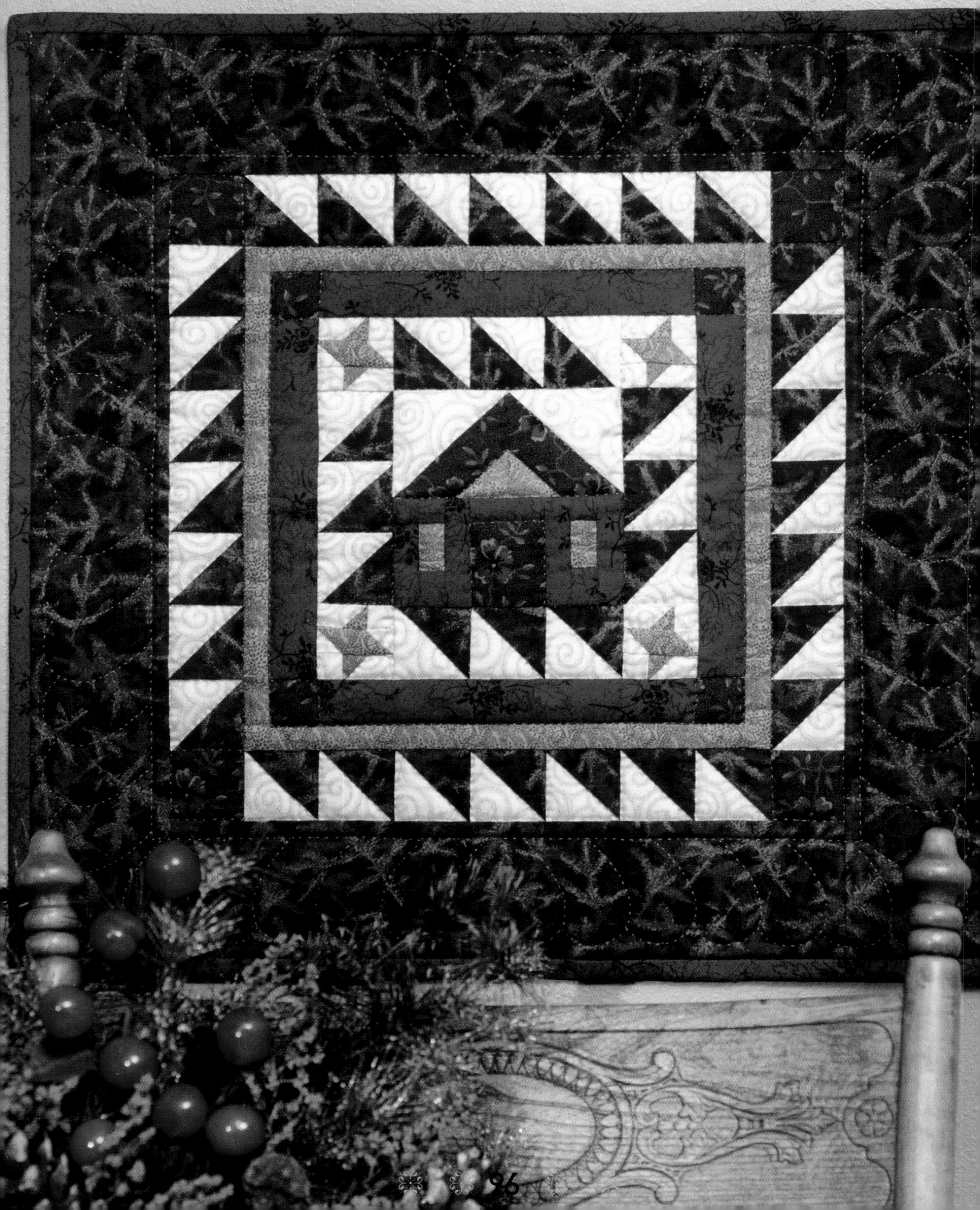

Winter & Winds

20-inches square

FABRICS AND SUPPLIES

1/3 yard BEIGE PRINT for background

1/8 yard BROWN PRINT for roof, door, and corner squares

1/8 yard GOLD PRINT for stars, windows, roof, and middle border

1/8 yard RED PRINT for house and inner border

3/8 yard GREEN PRINT for sawtooth borders and outer border

1/3 yard RED PRINT for binding

2/3 yard backing fabric

quilt batting, at least 24-inches square

House Block

Cutting

From **BEIGE PRINT**:
- Cut 1, 3-1/8-inch square

From **BROWN PRINT**:
- Cut 1, 3-1/8-inch square
- Cut 1, 2 x 2-1/4-inch rectangle

From **GOLD PRINT**:
- Cut 2, 1-1/2-inch squares
- Cut 2, 1 x 1-1/2-inch rectangles

From **RED PRINT**:
- Cut 1, 1 x 20-inch strip. From the strip cut:
    4, 1 x 2-3/4-inch rectangles
    1, 1 x 2-inch rectangle
    2, 1 x 1-1/4-inch rectangles
    2, 1-inch squares

Piecing

Step 1 With right sides together, layer the 3-1/8-inch **BEIGE** and **BROWN** squares. Press together, but do not sew. Cut the layered square in half diagonally to make 2 sets of triangles. Stitch 1/4-inch from the diagonal edge of each pair of triangles; press. <u>At this point each triangle-pieced square should measure 2-3/4-inches square.</u>

Make 2, 2-3/4-inch triangle-pieced squares

Step 2 With right sides together, position a 1-1/2-inch **GOLD** square on the **BROWN** corner of a triangle-pieced square. Draw a diagonal line on the **GOLD** square and stitch on the line. Trim the seam allowance to 1/4-inch; press. Make 2 pieced squares. Sew the 2 pieced squares together to make the roof unit. <u>At this point the roof unit should measure 2-3/4 x 5-inches.</u>

Make 2   Make 1

Step 3 To make the door unit, sew the 1 x 2-inch **RED** rectangle to the top edge of the 2 x 2-1/4-inch **BROWN** rectangle; press. <u>At this point the door unit should measure 2 x 2-3/4-inches.</u>

 Make 1

Step 4 To make the window units, sew a 1-inch **RED** square to the top edge of a 1 x 1-1/2-inch **GOLD** rectangle. Sew a 1 x 1-1/4-inch **RED** rectangle to the bottom edge of the **GOLD** rectangle; press. Sew 1 x 2-3/4-inch **RED** rectangles to both side edges of the unit; press. <u>At this point each window unit should measure 2 x 2-3/4-inches.</u>

Make 2   Make 2

Step 5 Sew the window units to both side edges of the door unit; press. <u>At this point the lower house unit should measure 2-3/4 x 5-inches.</u>

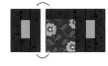 Make 1

Step 6 Sew together the roof unit and the lower house unit; press. <u>At this point the house block should measure 5-inches square.</u>

 Make 1

Star Blocks

Make 4 blocks

Cutting

From **GOLD PRINT**:
- Cut 4, 1 x 2-inch rectangles
- Cut 8, 1-inch squares

From **BEIGE PRINT**:
- Cut 1, 1 x 42-inch strip. From the strip cut:
    8, 1 x 1-1/2-inch rectangles
    16, 1-inch squares

Piecing

Step 1 Position a 1-inch **GOLD** square on the right corner of a 1 x 1-1/2-inch **BEIGE** rectangle. Draw a diagonal line on the square, stitch, trim, and press. Sew a 1-inch **BEIGE** square to the right edge of the unit; press.

   Make 8

Step 2 Position 1-inch **BEIGE** squares on both corners of a 1 x 2-inch **GOLD** rectangle. Draw a diagonal line on each square, stitch, trim, and press.

  Make 4

Step 3 Sew the Step 1 units to the top/bottom edges of the Step 2 units; press. <u>At this point each star block should measure 2-inches square.</u>

 Make 4

Sawtooth Borders

Cutting

From **BEIGE PRINT**:
- Cut 2, 2-3/8 x 42-inch strips

From **GREEN PRINT**:
- Cut 2, 2-3/8 x 42-inch strips

Piecing

Step 1 With right sides together, layer the 2-3/8 x 42-inch **BEIGE** and **GREEN** strips together in pairs. Press together, but do not sew. Cut the layered strips into squares. Cut the squares in half diagonally to make 40 triangle sets. Stitch 1/4-inch from the diagonal edge of each pair of triangles; press. <u>At this point each triangle-pieced square should measure 2-inches square.</u> Set 28 of the triangle-pieced squares aside to be used after the inner and middle borders are added.

 Crosscut 20, 2-3/8-inch squares

   Make 40, 2-inch triangle-pieced squares

Step 2 Sew 3 triangle-pieced squares together; press. Make 4 units. Sew a sawtooth unit to the top/bottom edges of the house block; press. Sew star blocks to both edges of the remaining sawtooth units; press. Sew the sawtooth/star units to the side edges of the house block; press. <u>At this point the quilt center should measure 8-inches square.</u>

Make 4

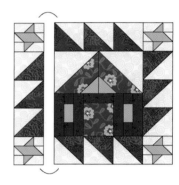
Make 1

Borders

Note: *The yardage given allows for the border strips to be cut on the crosswise grain. Read through **Border** instructions on page 118 for general instructions on adding borders.*

Cutting

From **RED PRINT**:
- Cut 1, 1-1/2 x 42-inch inner border strip

From **BROWN PRINT**:
- Cut 4, 2-inch corner squares
- Cut 4, 1-1/2-inch corner squares

From **GOLD PRINT**:
- Cut 2, 1 x 42-inch middle border strips

From **GREEN PRINT**:
- Cut 2, 3-1/2 x 42-inch outer border strips

Attaching the Borders

Step 1 Attach the 1-1/2-inch wide **RED** top/bottom inner border strips.

Step 2 For the side borders, measure the quilt center from top to bottom including the seam allowances but not the top and bottom borders. Cut the 1-1/2-inch wide **RED** side borders to this length. Sew 1-1/2-inch **BROWN** corner squares to both ends of the border strips; press. Sew the borders to the quilt center; press.

Step 3 Attach the 1-inch wide **GOLD** middle border strips.

Step 4 For the top/bottom sawtooth borders, sew together 7 of the triangle-pieced squares; press. Make 2 border strips. Sew the borders to the quilt center; press.

Make 2

Step 5 For the side sawtooth borders, sew together 7 of the triangle-pieced squares; press. Make 2 border strips. Sew 2-inch **BROWN** corner squares to both ends of the border strips; press. Sew the borders to the quilt center; press.

Make 2

Step 6 Attach the 3-1/2-inch wide **GREEN** outer border strips.

Putting It All Together

Trim the backing and batting so they are 4-inches larger than the quilt top. Refer to **Finishing the Quilt** on page 118 for complete instructions.

Binding

Cutting

From **RED PRINT**:
• Cut 3, 2-3/4 x 42-inch strips

Sew the binding to the quilt using a 3/8-inch seam allowance. This measurement will produce a 1/2-inch wide finished double binding. Refer to **Binding** and **Diagonal Piecing** on page 119 for complete instructions.

Winter Winds
20-inches square

Tea Time

Tea Time

16-inches square

FABRICS AND SUPPLIES

5 x 20-inch rectangle GREEN DIAGONAL PRINT for tea pot appliques

1/4 yard BEIGE PRINT for applique foundation and inner border

1/8 yard RED FLORAL for corner squares

1/4 yard GREEN/ROSE FLORAL for outer border

6-inch square ROSE PRINT for flower appliques

4-inch square GREEN PRINT for leaf and stem appliques

2-inch square GOLD PRINT for flower center appliques

1/2 yard RED PLAID for binding (cut on the bias)

5/8 yard backing fabric

quilt batting, at least 20-inches square

paper-backed fusible web

tear-away fabric stabilizer for applique (optional)

pearl cotton or machine-embroidery thread for decorative stitches; black

Tea Pot Blocks

Make 4 blocks

Cutting

From **BEIGE PRINT**:
- Cut 4, 4-1/2-inch applique foundation squares

From **RED FLORAL**:
- Cut 16, 1-1/2-inch squares

Applique - Fusible Web Method

Step 1 Position the fusible web, paper side up, over the applique shapes on page 105. With a pencil, trace the shapes onto fusible web the number of times indicated on the pattern pieces, leaving a small margin between each shape. Cut the shapes apart.

Step 2 Following the manufacturer's instructions, fuse the shapes to the wrong side of the fabric chosen for the appliques. Let the fabric cool and cut along the traced line. Peel away the paper backing from the fusible web.

Step 3 Referring to the block diagram, position the shapes on the 4-1/2-inch **BEIGE** squares; fuse in place.

Note: We suggest pinning a rectangle of tear-away stabilizer to the backside of the block to be appliqued so that it will lay flat when the applique is complete. We use the extra-light-weight Easy Tear™ sheets as a stabilizer. When the applique is complete, tear away the stabilizer.

Step 4 We machine buttonhole-stitched around the shapes using black Mettler® embroidery thread for the top thread and regular sewing thread in the bobbin. If you like, you could hand buttonhole-stitch around the shapes with pearl cotton.

Buttonhole Stitch

Tea Pot Assembly

Step 1 With right sides together, position a 1-1/2-inch **RED FLORAL** square on each corner of the tea pot blocks. Draw a diagonal line on the **RED FLORAL** squares. Stitch on the lines and trim seam allowances to 1/4-inch.

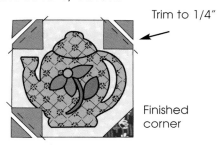

Trim to 1/4"

Finished corner

Step 2 Stitch the 4 tea pot blocks together; press.

Inner Border

Cutting

From **BEIGE PRINT**:
- Cut 1, 1-7/8 x 5-inch strip
- Cut 8, 1-1/2 x 4-1/2-inch rectangles

From **RED FLORAL**:
- Cut 1, 1-7/8 x 5-inch strip
- Cut 16, 1-1/2-inch squares

Piecing

Step 1 With right sides together, position a 1-1/2-inch **RED FLORAL** square on both ends of each of the 1-1/2 x 4-1/2-inch **BEIGE** rectangles. Draw a diagonal line on each square, stitch, trim and press.

Make 8

Step 2 Stitch the Step 1 units together in pairs; press. Sew a border to the top and bottom edges of the quilt center; press.

Make 4

Step 3 Layer the 1-7/8 x 5-inch **BEIGE** and **RED FLORAL** strips, right sides together. Press together, but do not sew. Cut the layered strip into 2, 1-7/8-inch squares. Cut the layered squares in half diagonally to make 4 sets of triangles. Stitch 1/4-inch from the diagonal edge of each pair of triangles; press.

   Make 4, 1-1/2-inch triangle-pieced squares

Step 4 Sew the triangle-pieced squares to both ends of the remaining borders. Sew the borders to the side edges of the quilt; press.

Make 2

Outer Border

Note: *The yardage given allows for the border strips to be cut on the crosswise grain. Read through* **Border** *instructions on page 118 for general instructions on adding borders.*

Cutting

From **GREEN/ROSE FLORAL**:
- Cut 2, 3-1/2 x 42-inch outer border strips

Attach the 3-1/2-inch wide **GREEN/ROSE FLORAL** outer border strips.

Putting It All Together

Trim the backing and batting so they are about 4-inches larger than the table topper. Refer to **Finishing the Quilt** on page 118 for complete instructions.

Binding

Cutting

From **RED PLAID**:
- Cut enough 2-3/4-inch wide **bias** strips to make a 75-inch long strip

Sew the binding to the quilt using a 3/8-inch seam allowance. This measurement will produce a 1/2-inch wide finished double binding. Refer to **Binding** and **Diagonal Piecing** on page 119 for complete instructions.

Placement Diagram

Tea Time
16-inches square

The applique shapes are reversed
for tracing purposes. When the
applique is finished it will appear as
in the photograph.

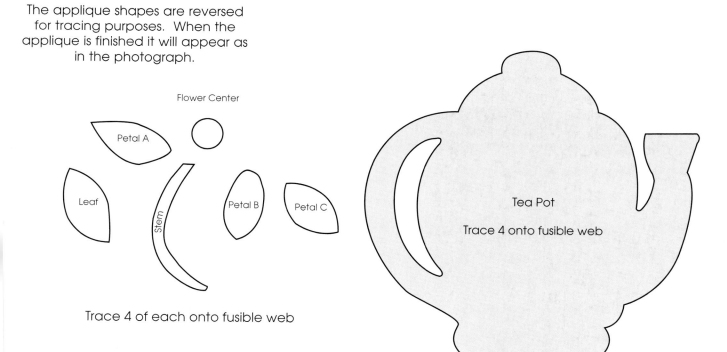

Flower Center

Petal A

Leaf

Stem

Petal B

Petal C

Tea Pot

Trace 4 onto fusible web

Trace 4 of each onto fusible web

Pine Berries

28-inches square

FABRICS AND SUPPLIES

5/8 yard BEIGE PRINT for background

1/4 yard GREEN PRINT #1 for trees

2 x 10-inch piece BROWN PRINT for tree trunks

1/4 yard BLUE FLORAL for dogtooth border

1/8 yard RED PRINT for corner squares and berry appliques

1/8 yard RED FLORAL for middle border

1/2 yard BLUE PRINT for outer border

1/4 yard GREEN PRINT #2 for stem/leaf appliques

3/8 yard RED PRINT for binding

7/8 yard backing fabric

1/2 yard freezer paper for leaf appliques

lightweight cardboard for berry appliques

template material

quilt batting, at least 32-inches square

Pine Tree Blocks

Make 4 blocks

Cutting

From **BEIGE PRINT:**
- Cut 8 of Pattern E
- Cut 4 of Pattern F
- Cut 12 of Pattern G
- Cut 12 of Pattern G reversed
- Cut 4 of Pattern H
- Cut 4 of Pattern H reversed

From **GREEN PRINT #1:**
- Cut 16 of Pattern A
- Cut 8 of Pattern B
- Cut 8 of Pattern C

From **BROWN PRINT:**
- Cut 4 of Pattern D

Piecing

Step 1   For one pine tree block you will need 4 **GREEN A** pieces, 2 **GREEN B** pieces, 2 **GREEN C** pieces, 1 **BROWN D** piece, 2 **BEIGE E** triangles, 1 **BEIGE F** triangle, 3 **BEIGE G** pieces, 3 **BEIGE G** reversed pieces, 1 **BEIGE H** piece, and 1 **BEIGE H** reversed piece.

Step 2   Referring to the diagram for placement, sew together a **BEIGE H** piece and a **GREEN A** piece. Press the seam allowance toward the **GREEN** fabric. In the same manner sew together:

a **GREEN B** piece to a **BEIGE G** piece
a **GREEN A** piece to a **BEIGE G** piece
a **GREEN C** piece to a **BEIGE G** piece
a **GREEN A** piece to a **BEIGE H** reversed piece
a **GREEN B** piece to a **BEIGE G** reversed piece
a **GREEN A** piece to a **BEIGE G** reversed piece
a **GREEN C** piece to a **BEIGE G** reversed piece

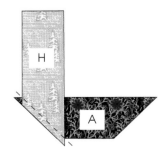

Step 3   Referring to the diagram for placement, sew together 4 pieced strips for each half of the tree. Press the seam allowances toward the top of the tree on the left-hand side and toward the bottom of the tree on the right-hand side. Sew together the 2 tree halves, stopping 1/4-inch from the end of the seam at the base of the tree. Backstitch at this point. Press the center seam allowance open.

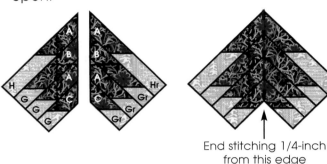

End stitching 1/4-inch
from this edge

Step 4   To make the trunk unit, sew a **BEIGE E** triangle to each long side of a **BROWN D** piece. Press the seam allowances toward the **BROWN** fabric. Sew the **BEIGE F** triangle to the bottom of the trunk unit; press.

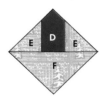

Step 5   Sew the trunk unit to the base of the tree. With right sides together, match the edge of the trunk unit with the **C/G** edge of the tree. Starting with the needle 1/4-inch in from the center top point of the trunk, stitch to the outer edge. Match the other edge of the trunk to the **C/G reversed** edge of the tree. Stitch 1/4-inch from the inner corner to the outer edge. <u>The blocks should measure approximately 5-inches square.</u>

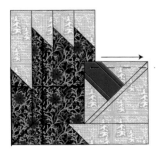

Make 4
tree blocks

Quilt Center

Note: *The corner triangles are larger than necessary and will be trimmed before the borders are added. You will be adding a pieced border so it is very important that your quilt center measures 15-1/2-inches square.*

Cutting

From **BEIGE PRINT:**
• Cut 2, 10-inch squares. Cut each square in half diagonally for a total of 4 corner triangles.

Quilt Center Assembly

Step 1 Sew the pieced tree blocks together in diagonal rows. Press the seam allowances in opposite directions. Sew the rows together; press.

Step 2 Center and sew the **BEIGE** corner triangles to two opposite sides of the quilt center; press. Center and add the remaining **BEIGE** corner triangles to the quilt center; press. Trim away the excess fabric from the corner triangles, taking care to allow 1-1/4-inches beyond the corners of each tree block so the tree blocks will appear to float. <u>At this point the quilt center should measure 15-1/2-inches square.</u>

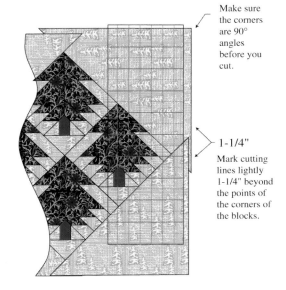

Make sure the corners are 90° angles before you cut.

1-1/4"
Mark cutting lines lightly 1-1/4" beyond the points of the corners of the blocks.

Applique the Quilt Center

Stem Applique

Cutting

From **GREEN PRINT #2:**
• Cut 4, 1-3/8 x 6-1/2-inch **bias** strips
• Cut 4, 1-3/8 x 3-1/2-inch **bias** strips

Step 1 Fold each strip in half lengthwise with wrong sides together; press. To keep the raw edges aligned, stitch a scant 1/4-inch away from the edges. Fold each strip in half again so the raw edges are hidden by the first folded edge; press.

Step 2 Referring to the quilt diagram, position the 3-1/2-inch long **GREEN** bias strips on the corners of the quilt center; pin in place. Applique the stems in place with matching thread. Tuck under the raw ends that will not be covered by the other applique pieces.

Step 3 Repeat Step 2 to add the 6-1/2-inch long **GREEN** bias strips.

Freezer Paper Applique - Leaf

With this method of hand applique, the freezer paper forms a base around which the leaf appliques are shaped.

Step 1 Make a template using the leaf pattern. Use a pencil to trace this shape 4 times onto the paper side of the freezer paper. Cut out the leaves on the traced lines.

Step 2 With a dry iron on the wool setting, press the coated side of each freezer paper leaf onto the wrong side of the fabric chosen for the applique. Allow at least 1/2-inch between each shape for seam allowances. Cut out each leaf a scant 1/4-inch beyond the edge of the freezer paper pattern.

Step 3 Referring to the quilt diagram, position a leaf applique on the quilt center and pin in place. With your needle, turn the seam allowance over the edge of the freezer paper and applique the shape in place with matching thread. When there is about 3/4-inch left to applique, slide your needle into this opening and loosen the freezer paper. Gently remove it and finish stitching the shape in place. Repeat with the remaining leaves.

Cardboard Applique - Berry

Step 1 Make a cardboard template using the berry pattern on page 111.

Step 2 Position the berry template on the wrong side of the fabric chosen for the applique and trace around the template 8 times, leaving a 3/4-

inch margin around each shape. Remove the template and cut a scant 1/4-inch beyond the drawn lines.

Step 3 To create smooth, round circles, run a line of basting stitches around the circle placing the stitches halfway between the drawn line and the cut edge of the circle. After basting, keep the needle and thread attached for the next step.

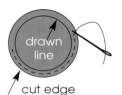 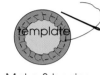

cut edge   Make 8 berries

Step 4 Place the cardboard template on the wrong side of the fabric circle and tug on the basting stitches, gathering the fabric over the template. When the thread is tight, space the gathers evenly and make a knot to secure the thread. Clip the thread, press the circle, and remove the cardboard template.

Step 5 Applique the berries to the quilt with matching thread.

Borders

Note: *The yardage given allows for the border strips to be cut on the crosswise grain. Diagonally piece the strips as needed, referring to* **Diagonal Piecing** *instructions on page 118. Read through* **Border** *instructions on page 118 for general instructions on adding borders.*

Cutting

From **BEIGE PRINT:**
- Cut 2, 2 x 42-inch strips. From the strips cut: 40, 2-inch squares

From **BLUE FLORAL:**
- Cut 2, 2 x 42-inch strips. From the strips cut: 20, 2 x 3-1/2-inch rectangles

From **RED PRINT:**
- Cut 4, 2-inch corner squares

From **RED FLORAL:**
- Cut 2, 1-1/2 x 42-inch middle border strips

From **BLUE PRINT:**
- Cut 3, 4-1/2 x 42-inch outer border strips

Attaching the Borders

Step 1 Position a 2-inch **BEIGE** square on the corner of a 2 x 3-1/2-inch **BLUE FLORAL** rectangle. Draw a diagonal line on the **BEIGE** square and stitch on the line. Trim the seam allowance to 1/4-inch. Press the seam allowance toward the **BLUE** fabric. Repeat this process at the opposite corner of the rectangle; press the seam allowance toward the **BEIGE** fabric.

Make 20

Step 2 Referring to the quilt diagram, sew together 5 of the Step 1 units for each of the dogtooth borders; press. At this point each dogtooth border strip should measure 2 x 15-1/2 inches. Sew 2 of the border strips to the top and bottom edges of the quilt center; press.

Step 3 Sew 2-inch **RED** corner squares to the remaining dogtooth border strips; press. Sew the border strips to the side edges of the quilt center; press.

Step 4 Attach the 1-1/2-inch wide **RED FLORAL** middle border strips.

Step 5 Attach the 4-1/2-inch wide **BLUE PRINT** outer border strips.

Putting It All Together

Trim the backing and batting so they are 4-inches larger than the quilt top. Refer to **Finishing the Quilt** on page 118 for complete instructions.

Binding

Cutting

From **RED PRINT:**
• Cut 4, 2-3/4 x 42-inch strips

Sew the binding to the quilt using a 3/8-inch seam allowance. This measurement will produce a 1/2-inch wide finished double binding. Refer to **Binding** and **Diagonal Piecing** on page 119 for complete instructions.

Pine Berries
28-inches square

The applique shapes are reversed for tracing purposes. When the applique is finished it will appear as in the diagram.

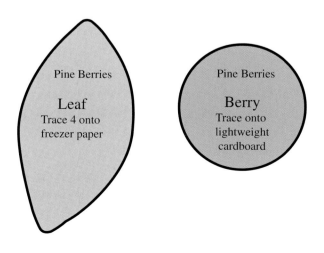

Pine Berries

Leaf
Trace 4 onto
freezer paper

Pine Berries

Berry
Trace onto
lightweight
cardboard

Pine Berries

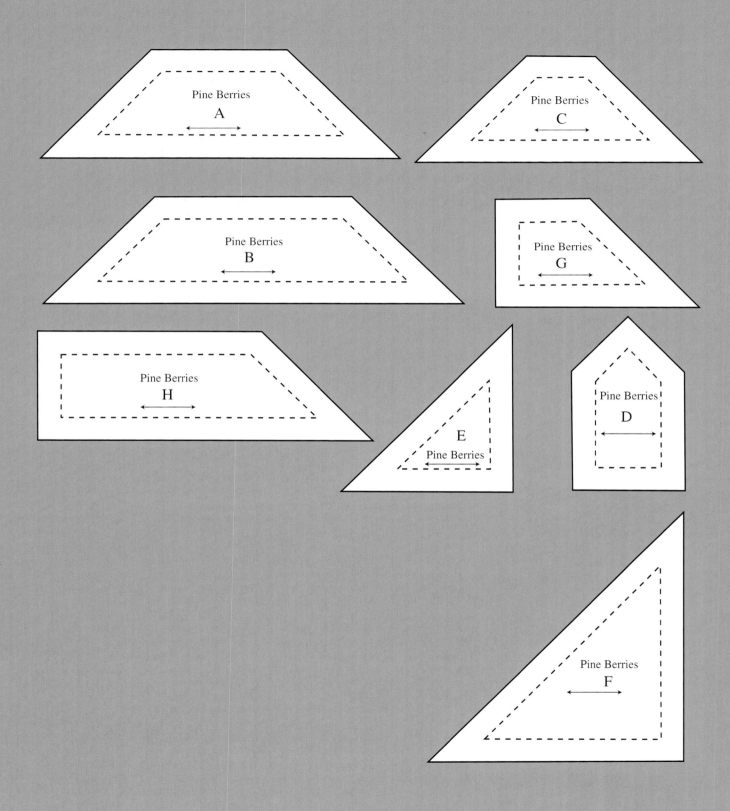

Pine Berries
Made Easy

21-inches square

Fabrics and Supplies

1/4 yard **BEIGE PRINT** for background

1/4 yard **GREEN PRINT #1** for trees

2 x 10-inch piece **BROWN PRINT** for tree trunks

1/3 yard **RED PRINT** for corner triangles

1/4 yard **GREEN PRINT #2** for border

1/3 yard **BLACK PRINT** for binding

3/4 yard backing fabric

quilt batting, at least 25-inches square

Corner triangles were quilted with the template from page 33 and crosshatching 1" apart.

- Refer to **Pine Berries** to cut and piece 4 tree blocks. Sew the tree blocks together; press.

- From **RED PRINT**:
  Cut 2, 10-inch squares.
  Cut each square in half diagonally for a total of 4 corner triangles.

- Referring to page 109, assemble the quilt center.

- From **GREEN PRINT #2**:
  Cut 2, 3-1/2 x 42-inch border strips

- Sew the **GREEN #2** border strip to the quilt center; press. Read through **Border** instructions on page 118 for general instructions on adding borders.

- Trim the backing and batting so they are 4-inches larger than the quilt top. Refer to **Finishing the Quilt** on page 119 for complete instructions.

- From **BLACK PRINT**:
  Cut 3, 2-3/4 x 42-inch binding strips

- Sew the binding to the quilt using a 3/8-inch seam allowance. This measurement will produce a 1/2-inch wide finished double binding. Refer to **Binding** and **Diagonal Piecing** on page 119 for complete instructions.

• Yardage is based on 42-inch wide fabric. If your fabric is wider or narrower it will affect the amount of necessary strips you need to cut in some patterns, and of course, it will affect the amount of fabric you have left over. Generally, THIMBLEBERRIES patterns allow for a little extra fabric so you can confidently cut your pattern pieces with ease.

• A rotary cutter, mat, and wide clear plastic ruler with 1/8-inch markings are needed tools in attaining accuracy. A beginner needs good tools just as an experienced quilt maker needs good equipment. A 24 x 36-inch mat board is a good size to own. It will easily accommodate the average quilt fabrics and will aid in accurate cutting. The plastic ruler you purchase should be at least 6 x 24-inches and easy to read. Do not purchase a smaller ruler to save money, the large size will be invaluable to your quilt making success.

• It is often recommended to prewash and press fabrics to test for color fastness and possible shrinkage. If you choose to prewash, wash in cool water and dry in a cool to moderate dryer. Industry standards actually suggest that line drying is best. Shrinkage is generally very minimal and usually is not a concern. A good way to test your fabric for both shrinkage and color fastness is to cut a 3-inch square of fabric. Soak the fabric in a white bowl filled with water. Squeeze the water out of the fabric and press it dry on a piece of muslin. If the fabric is going to release color it will do so either in the water or when it is pressed dry.

Re-measure the 3-inch fabric square to see if it has changed size considerably (more than 1/4-inch). If it has, wash, dry, and press the entire yardage. This little test could save you hours in prewashing and pressing.

• Read instructions thoroughly before beginning a project. Each step will make more sense to you when you have a general overview of the whole process. Take one step at a time and follow the illustrations. They will often make more sense to you than the words.

• For piecing, place right sides of the fabric pieces together and use 1/4-inch seam allowances throughout the entire quilt unless otherwise specifically stated in the directions. An accurate seam allowance is the most important part of the quilt making process after accurate cutting. All the directions are based on accurate 1/4-inch seam allowances. It is very important to check your sewing machine to see what position your fabric should be to get accurate seams. To test, use a piece of 1/4-inch graph paper, stitch along the quarter inch line as if the paper were fabric. Make note of where the edge of the paper lines up with your presser foot or where it lines up on the throat plate of your machine. Many quilters place a piece of masking tape on the throat plate to help guide the edge of the fabric. Now test your seam allowance on fabric. Cut 2, 2-1/2-inch squares, place right sides together and stitch along one edge. Press seam allowances in one direction and measure. At this point the unit should measure 2-1/2 x 4-1/2-inches. If it does not,

adjust your stitching guidelines and test again. Seam allowances are included in the cutting sizes given in this book.

• Pressing is the third most important step in quilt making. As a general rule, you should never cross a stitched seam with another seam unless it has been pressed. Therefore, every time you stitch a seam it needs to be pressed before adding another piece. It is very important that you press and not iron the seams. Pressing is a firm, up and down motion that will flatten the seams but not distort the piecing. Ironing is a back and forth motion and will stretch and distort the small pieces. Most quilters use steam to help the pressing process. The moisture does help and will not distort the shapes as long as the pressing motion is used.

Pressing Strip Sets

• When sewing strips of fabric together for strip sets, it is important to press the seam allowances nice and flat, usually to the dark fabric. Be careful not to stretch as you press, causing a "rainbow effect." This will affect the accuracy and shape of the pieces cut from the strip set. Press on the wrong side first with the strips perpendicular to the ironing board. Flip the piece over and press on the right side to prevent little pleats from forming at the seams. Laying the strip set lengthwise on the ironing board seems to encourage the rainbow effect, as shown in diagram.

rainbow effect

• An old fashioned rule is to press seam allowances in one direction, toward the darker fabric. Often, background fabrics are light in color and pressing toward the darker fabric prevents the seam allowances from showing through to the right side. Pressing seam allowances in one direction is thought to create a stronger seam. Also, for ease in hand-quilting, the quilting lines should fall on the side of the seam which is opposite the seam allowance. As you piece quilts, you will find these "rules" to be helpful but not necessarily always appropriate. Sometimes seams need to be pressed in the opposite direction so the seams of different units will fit together more easily which quilters refer to as seams "nesting" together. When sewing together two units with opposing seam allowances, use the tip of your seam ripper to gently guide the units under your presser foot. Sometimes it is necessary to re-press the seams to make the units fit together nicely. Always try to achieve the least bulk in one spot and accept that no matter which way you press, it may be a little tricky and it could be a little bulky.

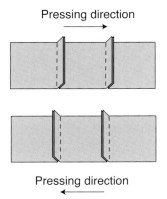

Pressing direction

Pressing direction

Squaring Up Blocks

To square up your blocks, first check the seam allowances. This is usually where the problem is, and it is always best to alter within the block rather than trim the outer edges. Next, make sure you have pressed accurately. Sometimes a block can become distorted by ironing instead of pressing.

• To trim up block edges, use one of many clear plastic squares available on the market. Determine the center of the block; mark with a pin. Lay the square over the block and align as many perpendicular and horizontal lines as you can to the seams in your block. This will indicate where the block is off. Do not trim all off on one side; this usually results in real distortion of the pieces in the block and the block design. Take a little off all sides until the block is square. When assembling many blocks, it it necessary to make sure *all* are the same size.

Tools and Equipment

Making beautiful quilts does not require a large number of specialized tools or expensive equipment. My list of favorites is short and sweet, and includes the things I use over and over again because they are always accurate and dependable.

• I find a long acrylic ruler indispensable for accurate rotary cutting. The ones I like most are an Omnigrid 6 x 24-inch grid acrylic ruler for cutting long strips and squaring up fabrics and quilt tops, and a Masterpiece 45, 8 x 24-inch ruler for cutting 6- to 8-inch wide borders. I sometimes tape together two 6 x 24-inch acrylic rulers for cutting borders up to 12-inches wide.

• A 15-inch Omnigrid square acrylic ruler is great for squaring up individual blocks and corners of a quilt top, for cutting strips up to 15-inches wide or long, and for trimming side and corner triangles.

• I think the markings on my 24 x 36-inch Olfa rotary cutting mat stay visible longer than on other mats, and the lines are fine and accurate.

• The largest size Olfa rotary cutter cuts through many layers of fabric easily, and it isn't cumbersome to use. The 2-1/2-inch blade slices through three layers of backing, batting, and a quilt top like butter.

• An 8-inch pair of Gingher shears is great for cutting out applique templates and cutting fabric from a bolt or fabric scraps.

• I keep a pair of 5-1/4-inch Gingher scissors by my sewing machine, so it is handy for both machine work and handwork. This size is versatile and sharp enough to make large and small cuts equally well.

• My Grabbit magnetic pin cushion has a surface that is large enough to hold lots of straight pins, and a strong magnet that keeps them securely in place.

• Silk pins are long and thin, which means they won't leave large holes in your fabric. I like them because they increase accuracy in pinning pieces or blocks together, and it is easy to press over silk pins, as well.

• For pressing individual pieces, blocks, and quilt tops, I use an 18 x 48-inch sheet of plywood covered with several layers of cotton fiberfill and topped with a layer of muslin stapled to the back. The 48-inch length allows me to press an entire width of fabric at one time without the need to reposition it, and the square ends are better than tapered ends on an ironing board for pressing finished quilt tops.

Rotary Cutting

• **Safety First!** The blades of a rotary cutter are very sharp and need to be for accurate cutting. Look at a variety of cutters to find one that feels good in your hand. All quality cutters have a safety mechanism to "close" the cutting blade when not in use. After each cut and before laying the rotary cutter down, close the blade. Soon this will become second nature to you and will prevent dangerous accidents. Always keep cutters out of the sight of children. Rotary cutters are very tempting to fiddle with when they are laying around. When your blade is dull or nicked, change it. Damaged blades do not cut accurately and require extra effort that can also result in slipping and injury. Also, always cut away from yourself for safety.

• Fold the fabric in half lengthwise matching the selvage edges.

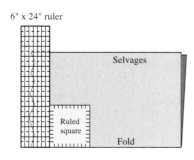

6" x 24" ruler

• "Square off" the ends of your fabric before measuring and cutting pieces. This means that the cut edge of the fabric must be exactly perpendicular to the folded edge which creates a 90° angle. Align the folded and selvage edges of the fabric with the lines on the cutting board, and place a ruled square on the fold. Place a 6 x 24-inch ruler against the side of the square to get a 90° angle. Hold the ruler in place, remove the square, and cut along the edge of the ruler. If you are left-handed, work from the other end of the fabric. Use the lines on your cutting board to help line up fabric, but not to measure and cut strips. Use a ruler for accurate cutting, always checking to make sure your fabric is lined up with horizontal and vertical lines on the ruler.

Cutting Strips

• When cutting strips or rectangles, cut on the crosswise grain. Strips can then be cut into squares or smaller rectangles.

• If your strips are not straight after cutting a few of them, refold the fabric, align the folded and selvage edges with the lines on the cutting board, and "square off" the edge again by trimming to straighten, and begin cutting.

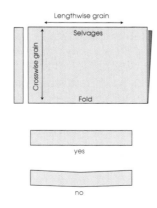

Cutting Side and Corner Triangles

In projects with side and corner triangles, the instructions have you cut side and corner triangles larger than needed. This will allow you to square up the quilt and eliminates the frustration of ending up with precut side and corner triangles that don't match the size of your pieced blocks.

To cut triangles, first cut squares. The project directions will tell you what size to make the squares and whether to cut them in half to make two triangles or to cut them in quarters to make four triangles, as shown in the diagrams. This cutting method will give you side triangles that have the straight of grain on the outside edges of the quilt. This is a very important part of quilt making that will help stabilize your quilt center.

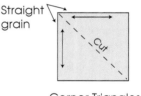

Corner Triangles

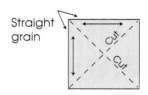

Side Triangles

ACCURATE TRIANGLES

Stitch on the outer edge just a "hair" or a thread width from the marked diagonal line.

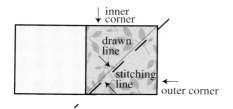

If you stitch on the inner corner side of the diagonal line you will actually make the triangle smaller.

"SQUARE" STRIP SETS

Make a habit of stopping often to check that your ruler is perpendicular to the strip set as you cross-cut your segments. Lining up a horizontal marking on your ruler with a strip set seam will help keep your segments "square."

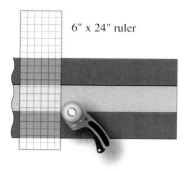

6" x 24" ruler

QUILTING SUGGESTIONS

• Repeat one of the design elements in the quilt as part of the quilting design.

• Two or three parallel rows of echo quilting outside an applique piece will highlight the shape.

• Stipple or meander quilting behind a feather or central motif will make the primary design more prominent.

• Look for quilting designs that will cover two or more borders, rather than choosing separate designs for each individual border.

• Quilting in the ditch of seams is an effective way to get a project quilted without a great deal of time marking the quilt.

CHAIN PIECING

To make the piecing process for "Downhill" more efficient, plan on chain piecing all of the left-hand "triangles" at one time. Clip, trim, and press; then repeat on the right-hand side of the rectangle.

MARKING THE QUILT DESIGN

When marking the quilt top, use a marking tool that will be visible on the quilt fabric and yet will be easy enough to remove. Always test your marking tool on a scrap of fabric before marking the entire quilt.

Along with a multitude of commerical marking tools available, you may find that very thin slivers of hand soap (Dial, Ivory, etc.) work really well for marking medium to dark color fabrics. The thin lines of soap show up nicely and the are easily removed by simply rubbing gently with a piece of like colored fabric.

Borders

Note . . .

The diagonal seams disguise the piecing better than straight seams. The exception is when a woven plaid is used for a border. It is then best to cut the border strips on the lengthwise grain (parallel to the selvages). When sewing on the bias, sew slowly and do not use too small of a stitch which could cause stretching of the fabric.

Diagonal Piecing

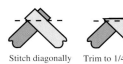

Stitch diagonally   Trim to 1/4" seam   Press seam open
            allowance

Step 1 With pins, mark the center points along all 4 sides of the quilt. For the top and bottom borders measure the quilt from left to right through the middle. This measurement will give you the most accurate measurement that will result in a "square" quilt.

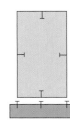

Step 2 Measure and mark the border lengths and center points on the strips cut for the borders before sewing them on.

Step 3 Pin the border strips to the quilt matching the pinned points on each of the borders and the quilt. Pin borders every 6 to 8-inches easing the fabric to fit as necessary. This will prevent the borders and quilt center from stretching while you are sewing them together. Stitch a 1/4-inch seam. Press the seam allowance toward the borders. Trim off excess border lengths.

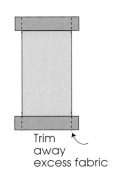

Trim away excess fabric

Step 4 For the side borders, measure your quilt from top to bottom, including the borders just added, to determine the length of the side borders.

Step 5 Measure and mark the side border lengths as you did for the top and bottom borders.

Step 6 Pin and stitch the side border strips in place. When attaching the last two side outer border strips, taking a few backstitches at the beginning and the end of the border will help keep the quilt borders intact during the quilting process. Press and trim the border strips even with the borders just added.

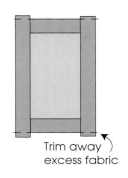

Trim away excess fabric

Step 7 If your quilt has multiple borders, measure, mark, and sew additional borders to the quilt in the same manner.

Finishing the Quilt

Now that your quilt is finished it needs to be layered with batting and backing, and prepared for quilting. Whether it is machine-quilted or hand-quilted, it is best to baste all 3 layers together. You may hand-baste with large basting stitches or pin-baste with medium size brass safety pins. Many quilters are satisfied with spray adhesives which are available at local quilt shops.

Step 1 Press the completed quilt top on the backside first, carefully clipping and removing hanging threads. Then press the quilt front making sure all seams are flat and all loose threads are removed.

Step 2 Remove the selvages from the backing fabric. Sew the long edges together; press. Trim the backing and batting so they are 4-inches larger than the quilt top.

Step 3 Mark the quilt top for quilting. Layer the backing, batting, and quilt top. Baste the 3 layers together and quilt. Work from the center of the quilt out to the edges. This will help keep the quilt flat by working the excess of the 3 layers to the outside edges.

Step 4 When quilting is complete, remove basting. Hand-baste the 3 layers together a scant 1/4-inch from the edge. This basting keeps the layers from shifting and prevents puckers from forming when adding the binding. Trim excess batting and backing fabric even with the edge of the quilt top.

Cutting Bias Binding

To cut bias binding strips, fold the binding yardage on the diagonal, forming a triangle. Using a rotary cutter, mat, and wide acrylic ruler, measure 1/2-inch from the fold, and cut away the folded edge to get a cut straight edge. Move the ruler across the fabric, cutting parallel strips in the desired binding width.

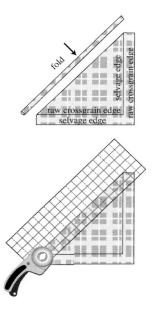

Diagonally piece the bias binding strips together, using as many long strips as possible, with shorter strips placed between the longer strips. Be careful not to stretch the seams as you stitch binding strips together.

The instructions for each quilt indicate the width to cut the binding used in that project. The measurements are sufficient for a quilt made of cotton quilting fabrics and medium low loft quilt batting. If you use a high loft batt or combine a fluffy high loft batt with flannel fabrics, you may want to increase the width of the binding strips by adding 1/4 to 1/2-inch to the cut width of your binding. Always test a small segment of the binding before cutting all the strips needed.

Stitch diagonally   Trim to 1/4" seam allowance   Press seam open

Step 1 Diagonally piece the binding strips. Fold the strip in half lengthwise, wrong sides together; press.

Double-Layer Binding

Step 2 Unfold and trim one end at a 45° angle. Turn under the edge 1/4-inch; press. Refold the strip.

Fold Line

Step 3 With raw edges of the binding and quilt top even, stitch with a 3/8-inch seam allowance, unless otherwise specified, starting 2-inches from the angled end.

Step 4 Miter the binding at the corners. As you approach a corner of the quilt, stop sewing 3/8 to 1-inch from the corner of the quilt (use the same measurement as your seam allowance). Generally, a 3/8-inch seam allowance is used for regular cotton quilts and often a 1-inch seam allowance is used for flannel quilts. Each project in this book gives specific instructions for the binding width and seam allowance to be used.

3/8" to 1"
Binding Strip
Quilt Top

Step 5 Clip the threads and remove the quilt from under the presser foot.

Step 6 Flip the binding strip up and away from the quilt, then fold the binding down even with the raw edge of the quilt. Begin sewing at the upper edge. Miter all 4 corners in this manner.

Quilt Top   Quilt Top

Step 7 Trim the end of the binding so it can be tucked inside of the beginning binding about 1/2-inch. Finish stitching the seam.

Quilt Top   Quilt Top

Step 8 Turn the folded edge of the binding over the raw edges and to the back of the quilt so that the stitching line does not show. Pin as needed to create a nice mitered corner on the back as well as on the front. Slip stitch the binding to the backside of the quilt by hand. To do this, slip your needle into the quilt back, sliding the needle approximately 1/4-inch. Bring it out of the fabric again and catch a few threads in the fold of the binding. At exactly the same point from which the needle emerged, insert it into the quilt back again, and take the next stitch.

Quilt Back   Quilt Back   Quilt Back

Thank you to the Staff of Thimbleberries® Design Studio:
Sue Bahr, Lisa Kirchoff, Kathy Lobeck, Ardelle Paulson,
Sherry Husske, Virginia Brodd, Renae Ashwill,
Julie Jergens, Tracy Schrantz, Clarine Howe,
Pearl Baysinger, Ellen Carter, and
quilters Julie Borg, and Leone Rusch.

Published by
Publishing Solutions, LLC
1107 Hazeltine Boulevard
Suite 470
Chaska, MN 55318
952-361-4902
James L. Knapp, President
www.ipubsolutions.com

Several people provided significant support in the publication
of this edition of THIMBLEBERRIES® PINT-SIZE TRADITIONS.
A special thank you to: Lynette Jensen of Thimbleberries®; Hank Toolan,
Kim Vivas and Tony Grega at Creative Homeowner®,
Laurel Albright of LA Studios; and Carmen McMeen
at Publishing Solutions, LLC.

Cover Design by Laurel Albright

Production Management Book Productions, LLC

1 2 3 4 5 6 7 8 9 10